IN THIS TIME OF
EXTREME DANGER

Northern Virginia
in the
American Revolution

Michael Cecere

HERITAGE BOOKS

2006

HERITAGE BOOKS

AN IMPRINT OF HERITAGE BOOKS, INC.

Books, CDs, and more—Worldwide

For our listing of thousands of titles see our website
at
www.HeritageBooks.com

Published 2006 by
HERITAGE BOOKS, INC.
Publishing Division
65 East Main Street
Westminster, Maryland 21157-5026

International Standard Book Number: 978-0-7884-4304-6

Contents

Maps

Acknowledgements

I am immensely grateful to Marguerite Knickmeyer, my teaching partner and friend, for her editorial assistance and support. I am also indebted to Rob Friar, my friend and fellow re-enactor in the 7th Virginia Regiment for his knowledge and input on the events of 1781 in southern Virginia.

Institutions that provided valuable research help included, the Simpson Library at the University of Mary Washington, the Handley Regional Library in Winchester, Virginia, the David Library in Washington's Crossing, Pennsylvania, and the Library of Congress.

Lastly, I want to thank my wife, Susan, and my children, Jenny and Michael, for their continued support.

Chapter One

"Our All is at Stake"
1764-1773

The first hint of trouble for the American colonists came in the fall of 1764 when rumors of Parliament's new stamp tax began to circulate. The colonists were accustomed to paying taxes on a few imported goods. It was Britain's way of regulating trade and was accepted by the colonies as the price of membership in the British Empire. Never before, however, had Parliament directly taxed the colonies to raise revenue. If the rumors were true, the stamp tax would establish a dangerous new precedent, taxation without representation.

In December 1764, a few members of Virginia's legislative assembly, the House of Burgesses, tried to head off the tax with a petition to King George III. The petitioners pledged their loyalty to the King but politely reminded him that,

> It [is] *a fundamental Principle of the British Constitution, without which Freedom can no Where exist, that the People are not subject to any Taxes but such as are laid on them by their own Consent, or by those legally appointed to represent them....*[1]

They claimed that since there were no colonial representatives in Parliament, that body had no authority to tax them.

---

[1] William Van Schreeven and Robert L. Scribner, ed., "Address, Memorial, and Remonstrance of the General Assembly to King, Lords, and Commons Respectively in Opposition to a Proposed Stamp Tax, 18 December, 1764," *Revolutionary Virginia: The Road to Independence, Vol. 1*, (Charlottesville: University Press of Virginia, 1973), 11

In London, financial concerns outweighed constitutional rights, and the Stamp Act was passed by Parliament in 1765. The act required the colonists to use stamped paper for legal documents, diplomas, newspapers, and even playing cards. The revenue generated by the tax would help defray future British military expenses in the colonies.

The amount of the tax was inconsequential to the colonists. They were upset about the dangerous precedent the tax established. If Parliament was allowed to levy a stamp tax today, what would prevent it from passing more laws or taxes tomorrow? With no representation in Parliament, the colonists were powerless to influence legislation. They were at the mercy of men who lived 3,000 miles away; men who knew little about life in North America.

This threat to their long established tradition of local autonomy prompted many colonists to vigorously object to the stamp act. Colonel George Washington, of Fairfax County, noted that Virginians,

> *Look upon this unconstitutional method of Taxation as a direful attack upon their Liberties, and loudly exclaim against the Violation.*[2]

Washington suggested that the colonists reduce trade with Britain to protest the tax. He believed such action would quickly impact England's economy and focus Parliament's attention on colonial grievances.[3] A boycott would also force the colonists to become more frugal and resourceful and, therefore, less dependent on British manufacturers:

---

[2] W.W. Abbot and Dorothy Twohig, eds. "George Washington to Francis Dandridge, 20 September, 1765," *The Papers of George Washington: Colonial Series, Vol. 7,* (Charlottesville: University Press of Virginia, 1990), 395-396
[3] Ibid.

Washington noted that,

> *The Eyes of our People, already beginning to open, will perceive, that many Luxuries [from] Great Britain...can well be dispensed with whilst the necessaries of Life are (mostly) to be had within ourselves. This consequently will introduce frugality, and be a necessary stimulation to Industry.*[4]

Another Virginian, Patrick Henry of Hanover County, created an uproar in Williamsburg when he proposed a series of resolutions in the House of Burgesses that challenged Parliament's authority. While conservative members cried treason, Henry convinced the House to adopt five resolutions. The most controversial one stated that the power to tax rested with Virginia's elected representatives, not the British Parliament:

> *The General Assembly of this Colony have the only and exclusive Right and Power to lay Taxes...upon the inhabitants of this Colony and that every Attempt to vest such Power in any person or persons other than the General Assembly has a manifest Tendency to destroy British as well as American Freedom.*[5]

---

[4] Ibid.

[5] Van Schreeven and Scribner, "Resolutions Offered by Patrick Henry in Condemnation of the Stamp Act, 29-30 May, 1765," *Revolutionary Virginia: The Road to Independence, Vol. 1,* 18

Stamp Act Repealed

Opposition to the Stamp Act spread throughout the colonies in 1765. It occurred in a variety of forms, some peaceful and some not so peaceful. However, it was not colonial opposition, but the arguments of prominent members of Parliament that persuaded that body to repeal the tax in 1766. Virginians learned of the happy news through published letters in the Virginia Gazette. Many of the letters urged the colonists not to gloat over their success:

> *Blessed to God the act is repealed, after a terrible struggle. O that Boston, that America may be truly thankful and humble, and frugal, and not insult the parliament in their rejoicings for this would render you odious to those who have been your firm friends.*[6]

Another letter encouraged the colonists to be grateful for Parliament's decision:

> *Prevail upon them* [the colonists] *to mix discretion with this great joy, that you do not exult as conquerors, but receive the blessing (now confirmed to you) with thankfulness and gratitude.*[7]

George Mason, of Fairfax County, resented the idea that the colonists should be grateful to Parliament for reversing something that was wrong in the first place. In June 1766, he wrote to a committee of merchants in London to assert that the

---

[6] "Extract of a letter from a Rev. Divine in London dated March 3, 1766," Purdie & Dixon, *Virginia Gazette*, 23 May, 1766, 2

[7] "Extract of a letter from a Gentleman in London to his friend in New York dated February 27," Purdie & Dixon, *Virginia Gazette*, 23 May, 1766, 2

American colonists were fellow Britons who valued their rights as much as the inhabitants of Great Britain:

> *Let our fellow-subjects in Great Britain reflect that we are descended from the same stock with themselves, nurtured in the same principles of freedom...that in crossing the Atlantic Ocean, we have only changed our climate, not our minds, our natures and dispositions remain unaltered; that we are still the same people with them in every respect; only not yet debauched by wealth, luxury, venality, and corruption....*[8]

Mason claimed that the colonists possessed the same rights and privileges as native Britons, rights that they expected to pass on to their children:

> *We claim nothing but the liberty and privileges of Englishmen, in the same degree, as if we still [lived] among our brethren in Great Britain; these rights have not been forfeited by any act of ours; we cannot be deprived of them, without our consent, but by violence and injustice; we have received them from our ancestors, and, with God's leave, we will transmit them, unimpaired, to our posterity.*[9]

Such bold claims troubled many members of Parliament. Stung by the strong opposition to the stamp act, Parliament decided to reassert its authority over the colonies. The Declaratory Act of 1766 boldly claimed that Parliament and the King had the authority to rule the colonies:

---

[8] Robert A. Rutland, ed., "To the Committee of Merchants in London, 6 June, 1766," *The Papers of George Mason, Vol. 1*, (University of North Carolina Press, 1970), 68

[9] Ibid.

The Declaratory Act : 1766

The said colonies...in America have been, are, and of right ought to be, subordinate unto, and dependent upon the imperial crown and Parliament of Great Britain; and that the king...with the advice and consent of...Parliament...hath...full power and authority to make laws...to bind the colonies and people of America, subjects of the crown of Great Britain, in all cases whatsoever.[10]

Most colonists rejected the premise of the Declaratory Act and reacted to it with ambivalence because Parliament did not actually exercise its newly defined authority. This changed in 1767 with the passage of the Townshend Duties. Parliament added new duties (taxes) to a long list of imported British goods like tea, glass, paint, and paper. The British Ministry claimed that since the colonists had historically paid duties on certain imports, they could not constitutionally oppose such taxes. The colonists countered with the argument that the earlier duties were designed to regulate trade, but the Townshend Duties were clearly designed to raise revenue for Great Britain. They appealed to Parliament to rescind the new taxes, but their pleas were ignored.

Non-Importation Association : 1769

By 1769 many colonists, including George Washington, were frustrated at Parliament's refusal to redress colonial grievances. Washington believed the colonies had to press their opposition with more force. On April 5th, 1769 he shared this view with his friend, George Mason:

---

[10] Henry Steele Commager, "The Declaratory Act, 18 March, 1766," *Documents of American History*, (New York: Appleton-Century-Crofts, 1963), 60-61

*At a time when our lordly Masters in Great Britain
will be satisfied with nothing less than the
deprivation of American freedom, it seems highly
necessary that some thing shou'd be done to avert the
stroke and maintain the liberty which we have
derived from our Ancestors....*[11]

Washington added that it was every man's duty to defend his
freedom with force if necessary. But such force should only
be used as a last resort.[12] He suggested to Mason that a
boycott of British goods was the next logical step for the
colonies:

*Addresses to the Throne, and remonstrances to
Parliament, we have already...proved the inefficacy
of; how far then [will] their attention to our rights &
priviledges...be awakened or alarmed by starving
their Trade & manufacture? The northern Colonies,
it appears, are endeavouring to adopt this
scheme...Upon the whole...I think the Scheme a good
one, and that it ought to be tried here....*[13]

Mason replied to Washington the same day. He supported a
boycott and proclaimed that he was ready to sacrifice the
"comforts of life" to preserve his liberty:

*Our All is at Stake, & the little Conveniencys &
Comforts of Life, when set in Competition with our
Liberty, ought to be rejected not with Reluctance but
with Pleasure....*[14]

---

[11] Rutland, "George Washington to George Mason, 5 April, 1769," *The
Papers of George Mason, Vol. 1,* 96-98
[12] Ibid.
[13] Ibid.
[14] Rutland, "George Mason to George Washington, 5 April, 1769," *The
Papers of George Mason, Vol. 1,* 99

Mason was confident that a boycott would quickly get Britain's attention and cause English manufacturers to pressure Parliament to address American complaints:

> *We may* [reject] *all Manner of* [English] *Finery... & confine ourselves to* [home grown] *Linnens and Woolens...It is amazing how much this (if adopted in all the Colonys) wou'd lessen American Imports, and distress the various Traders & Manufacturers in Great Britain – This wou'd quickly awaken their Attention – they wou'd see, they wou'd feel the Oppressions we groan under, & exert themselves to procure us Redress.*[15]

Mason drafted a boycott plan and sent it with Washington to the House of Burgesses in Williamsburg. The Burgesses prepared to discuss Mason's proposal in late May, but were thwarted when Governor Botetourt dissolved the assembly. Undeterred by Botetourt's action, the dismissed burgesses met at a nearby tavern to discuss Mason's plan. They approved most of Mason's proposals and urged all of the colonists to, *"promote & encourage Industry & Frugality & discourage all manner of Luxury & Extravigance."*[16] Ninety-four burgesses, including Henry Lee II and Foushee Tebbs of Prince William County, Francis Peyton and Thomson Mason of Loudoun County, and George Washington of Fairfax County joined a voluntary association to boycott the taxed items.[17] Within a year other colonies implemented similar boycotts.

Although many colonists violated the boycott, the level of trade with Britain noticeably declined. By the spring of 1770, Parliament grudgingly relented to the economic pressure and

---

[15] Ibid.

[16] Van Schreeven and Scribner, "Non-importation Resolutions of the Former Burgesses, 18 May, 1769," *Revolutionary Virginia: The Road to Independence, Vol. 1,* 75

[17] Ibid. 76-77

repealed all of the Townshend duties except the tax on tea. They defiantly maintained that duty to assert their right to tax the colonies. The colonists responded by lifting the boycott on everything except tea.

In 1773, Parliament tried to induce the colonists to break the tea boycott with the passage of the Tea Act. On the surface the new law appeared to benefit the colonists. The British East India Company was allowed to bypass colonial merchants and sell its taxed tea directly to the colonists at a significantly lower price than smuggled Dutch tea. The question was, would the colonists violate their principles and buy cheaper English tea despite the tax on it. Boston gave its answer on December 16th, when scores of Bostonians dumped a shipment of tea into the harbor. This action outraged Parliament and the King. They interpreted it as a blatant challenge to their authority and responded forcefully.

Chapter Two

"We Shall Not Suffer Ourselves to be Sacrificed by Piece Meals" 1774

The first reports of the Boston Tea Party reached Virginia in mid-January, nearly a month after the incident. Criticism of the Bostonians soon followed. One writer to the *Virginia Gazette* observed that,

> *The Lives of the* [Tea] *commissioners* [have] *been notoriously threatened and their Properties notoriously invaded at Boston, by a Set of lawless Rioters...Is there no Danger to Liberty when every Merchant is liable to have his House, Property, and even Life, invaded or threatened by a Mob, who may be assembled at any Time....*[1]

James Madison, of Orange County, congratulated a friend in Philadelphia on the peaceful way that city rejected a similar shipment of tea. Madison wished that, "*Boston* conduct[ed] *matters with as much discretion....*"[2]

Few Virginians supported the destruction of private property in Boston, yet some blamed Britain for the unrest. A letter in the Virginia Gazette noted that,

> *By all Accounts from New England, the people are in such a Ferment about the Tax upon Tea...The Conduct of* [Parliament] *towards all our Colonies,*

---

[1] Purdie & Dixon, *Virginia Gazette*, 20 January, 1774
[2] Gaillard Hunt, ed., "James Madison to William Bradford Jr., 24 January 1774," *The Writings of James Madison, Vol. 1*, (NY: G.P. Putnam's Sons, 1900), 18

*has been highly detrimental and injurious...This is
the Source and Foundation of all the Uneasiness and
Disturbances which have arisen....*[3]

Storm from the North

Although the uproar about the Tea Party subsided in the
spring, the issue erupted again in mid-May when Parliament's
response reached the colonies. The Virginia House of
Burgesses was interrupted by the stunning news of
Parliament's crackdown on Massachusetts.

In a series of laws dubbed the Intolerable Acts by the
colonists, Parliament abolished the Massachusetts Assembly
and placed the colony under martial law. Boston was
particularly affected by the Port Bill, which closed Boston
Harbor and destroyed the livelihood of hundreds of people.

The Intolerable Acts dominated the attention of Virginians.
George Mason, one of two members of the House of
Burgesses from Fairfax County, noted that, *"every body's
attention* [is] *entirely engrossed by the Boston affair....*[4]
Mason joined a committee of burgesses, including Patrick
Henry and Thomas Jefferson, to draft a resolution in support
of the people of Boston. It was Mason's first meeting with
Patrick Henry, and he was very impressed by the gentleman:

> *He is by far the most powerful speaker I ever heard.
> Every word he says not only engages but commands
> the attention; and your passions are no longer your
> own when he addresses them. But his eloquence is
> the smallest part of his merit. He is in my opinion the
> first man upon the continent, as well in abilities as
> public virtues....*[5]

---

[3] Purdie & Dixon, *Virginia Gazette*, 5 May, 1774
[4] Rutland, "George Mason to Martin Cockburn, 26 May, 1774," *The
Papers of George Mason: 1725-1792, Vol. 1*, 190
[5] Ibid.

The committee tried to draft a resolution that would not provoke Governor Dunmore to dissolve the Assembly. They called for a day of fasting, humiliation, and prayer for the people of Boston. The burgesses approved the resolution on May 24th, and proclaimed the first day of June to be the day of observance.

Lord Dunmore believed the resolution insulted the King and Parliament and dissolved the House of Burgesses on May 26th. A frustrated George Washington, the other burgess from Fairfax County, was angered by Dunmore's action because it prevented the colony from conducting important governmental business.[6]

Washington expressed the view of many Virginians when he declared to his friend, George Fairfax that,

> *The* [British] *Ministry may rely on it that Americans will never be tax'd without their own consent....*[7]

He also told Fairfax that Boston's plight was the plight of all the colonies, and that the colonists would never allow Britain to divide and conquer them:

> *The cause of Boston...is and ever will be considered as the cause of America (not that we approve their conduct in destroyg. the Tea)...we shall not suffer ourselves to be sacrificed by piece meals....*[8]

Colonel Washington was concerned with more than just the crisis in Boston. Reports of Indian raids on the frontier compounded his anxiety.

---

[6] Beverly Runge, ed., "George Washington to George William Fairfax, 10-15 June, 1775," *The Papers of George Washington: Colonial Series, Vol. 10*, 96

[7] Ibid.

[8] Ibid.

> *"God only knows what is to become of us,"* he
> lamented to Fairfax, *"threatned as we are with so
> many...evils as hang over us at present; having a
> cruel and blood thirsty Enemy upon our Backs, the
> Indians...with whom a general War is inevitable...."*[9]

Aggravating the situation was the fact that the very people
Virginians looked to for help against the Indians were
themselves threatening their liberty. Washington complained
to Fairfax that,

> *Those from whom we have a right to seek protection
> [Parliament] are endeavouring by every piece of Art
> and despotism to fix the Shackles of Slavery upon
> us.*[10]

He concluded his letter pessimistically:

> *In short since the first Settlemt of this Colony the
> Minds of People...never were more disturbd, or our
> Situation so critical as at present; arising...from an
> Invasion of our Rights and Priviledges by the Mother
> Country; and our lives and properties by the
> Savages....*[11]

---

[9] Ibid.
[10] Ibid.
[11] Ibid.

Virginia Rallies to Boston's Side

Many of the dismissed burgesses refused to be intimidated by the Governor and gathered at the Raleigh Tavern, near the capitol, to discuss ways to support Massachusetts. On May 27th, eighty-nine former burgesses, including George Washington of Fairfax County, Francis Peyton of Loudoun County, and Henry Lee II of Prince William County, declared that Parliament's crackdown on Massachusetts was a grievous violation of the British constitution and was designed to enslave the colonists.

With much grief we find that our dutiful applications to Great Britain for security of our just, ancient, and constitutional rights, have been not only disregarded, but that a determined system is formed and pressed for reducing the inhabitants of British America to slavery, by subjecting them to the payment of taxes, imposed without consent of the people or their representatives; and that in pursuit of this system, we find an act of the British parliament, lately passed, for stopping the...commerce of the town of Boston...until the people there submit to the payment of such unconstitutional taxes...a most dangerous attempt to destroy the constitutional liberty and rights of all North America....[12]

The former burgesses accused the East India Company of collusion in the plot to deprive the colonies of their rights and pledged to boycott all of the company's goods (except spices and saltpeter). [13]

---

[12] Van Schreeven and Scribner, "An Association Signed by 89 Members of the late House of Burgesses, 27 May 1774," *Revolutionary Virginia: The Road to Independence, Vol. 1,* 97-98

[13] Ibid.

The ex-burgesses concluded with a call for colonial unity.

> *We are further clearly of opinion, that an attack, made on one of our sister colonies, to compel submission to arbitrary taxes, is an attack made on all British America, and threatens ruin to the rights of all, unless the united wisdom of the whole be applied. And for this purpose it is recommended...* [that] *deputies from the several colonies of British America meet in general congress.* [14]

Most of the burgesses left Williamsburg the next day, satisfied with their bold action. On May 29th, however, the Virginia Committee of Correspondence received letters from the northern colonies that proposed even stronger measures. The chairman of the committee, Peyton Randolph, called the former burgesses back to Williamsburg to discuss the proposals. George Washington and Henry Lee II were still in the capital as was Thomas Blackburn, the other Prince William representative. They joined twenty-two other ex-burgesses (all that could be gathered at such short notice) in support of a continental boycott of British goods, (pending approval from the rest of their fellow representatives).[15] To obtain this approval, the ex-burgesses instructed each county to send representatives to a special meeting in Williamsburg on the first day of August. This meeting, or convention, would select Virginia's delegates to a general congress in Philadelphia.

---

[14] Ibid.
[15] Van Schreeven and Scribner, *Revolutionary Virginia, Vol. 1*, 99-100

The County Resolves

While these events occurred in Williamsburg, the counties in northern Virginia boldly expressed their views on the dispute. On May 31st, a committee in the town of Dumfries, (a thriving tobacco port and the commercial center of Prince William County) called the county's freeholders to a special meeting at the courthouse. The committee consisted of most of the county's leaders, including, Cuthbert Bullitt, William Grayson, Foushee Tebbs, Richard Graham, and Andrew Leitch. It called on the county's freeholders to

> *Deliberate on Measures...to be taken to avert the dreadful Calamities which...are threatened from the unconstitutional Act of Parliament* [and which] *is fundamentally subversive of our ancient legal and vital Liberties.*[16]

They met a week later, on June 6th, and passed a set of resolves that re-asserted the principle of no taxation without representation and claimed that Massachusetts was being punished for defending that principle. The freeholders then called for economic measures to pressure Britain to change its policy.

---

[16] Van Schreeven and Scribner, "Meeting of the Inhabitants of the Town of Dumfries, 31 May, 1774," *Revolutionary Virginia, Vol. 2*, 93

18

Prince William County Resolves June 6, 1774

Resolved...that no person ought to be taxed but by his own consent, expressed either by himself, or his representatives, and that therefore any act of parliament, levying a tax to be collected in America, depriving the people of their property, or prohibiting them from trading with one another, is subversive of our natural rights, and contrary to the first principles of our constitution.

Resolved, that the city of Boston...is now suffering in the common cause of American liberty, and on account of its opposition to an act of the British legislature for imposing a duty upon tea to be collected in America...

Resolved...until the said acts are repealed, all importation from, and exportation to, this colony ought to be stopped, except with such colonies or islands in North America as shall adopt this measure.[17]

A week later the freeholders of Loudoun County expressed their own displeasure with Parliament. They assembled at the county courthouse in Leesburg on June 14th, to consider,

The most effectual method to preserve the rights and liberties of N. America and relieve our brethren of Boston, suffering under the most oppressive tyrannical Act of the British Parliament.[18]

---

[17] Rutland, "Prince William County Resolves, 6 June, 1774," *The Papers of George Mason, Vol. 1*, 101

[18] Brent Tarter and Robert L. Scribner, "Loudoun County Resolves," *Revolutionary Virginia: The Road to Independence, Vol. 7, part 2* (University Press of Virginia, 1983), 733-734

The result of the meeting was the Loudoun County Resolves. They reaffirmed the principle of no taxation without representation and claimed that Parliament's crackdown on Massachusetts was a *"despotic exertion of unconstitutional power."* The resolves pledged support for *"our suffering brethren of Boston"* and advocated a boycott of British goods until Parliament altered its oppressive policies.

Loudoun County Resolves June 14, 1774

Resolved, That it is beneath the dignity of freemen to submit to any tax not imposed on them in the usual manner, by representatives of their own choosing.

Resolved, That the Act of the British Parliament...is utterly repugnant to the fundamental laws of justice, in punishing persons without even the form of a trial; [It is] a despotic exertion of unconstitutional power...calculated to enslave a free and loyal people.

Resolved, That the enforcing of the...act of Parliament by [the military threatens] civil war, and that we will, with our lives and fortunes, assist and support our suffering brethren of Boston...until a redress of all our grievances shall be procured, and our common liberties established on a permanent foundation.

Resolved, That we will have no commercial [trade] with Great Britain until the...Act of Parliament shall be totally repealed, and the right of regulating the internal policy of N. America by a British Parliament shall be absolutely and positively given up.[19]

---

[19] Ibid.

Moderates Urge Caution

Not every Virginian agreed with these resolves, especially the call for a boycott. In early July, Bryan Fairfax, a good friend of George Washington, wrote to Mount Vernon and expressed his opposition to a boycott of British goods. He considered such an act provocative and difficult to implement and urged Virginia to send another petition to England instead:

> *I should think Myself bound to oppose violent Measures now. The Entering upon a Plan of having no Trade would be an arduous Undertaking...I therefore think it would be more proper to try what Effect a petition might have towards obtaining a repeal of the Duty.* [20]

Fairfax worried that a boycott would only anger Parliament and undermine any chance of a repeal of the Intolerable Acts.

> *I would willingly give the Parliament a fair Opportunity to* [repeal the acts], *and therefore should be for a petition unaccompanied with any Threats or Claims (for we have already used them) and if such an Opportunity should be missed, we might then be better able to judge of* [Parliament's] *real Intention towards us.* [21]

Fairfax agreed that Parliament had no right to tax the colonies, but doubted that a boycott could be effectively implemented:

---

[20] Runge, "Bryan Fairfax to George Washington, 3 July, 1774," *The Papers of George Washington: Colonial Series, Vol. 10,* 107-108
[21] Ibid.

In opposing [Parliament] *we should consider all the Consequences that may follow. Threats at this time...will have no Effect...For which reason I am for postponing* [a threat of a boycott] *till the Effect of a Petition be first tryed....*[22]

George Washington was skeptical of Fairfax's position. He maintained that a boycott was overdue:

As to your political sentiments, I would heartily join you in them...provided there was the most distant hope of success. But have we not tried this already? Have we not addressed [Parliament] *? And to what end? Did they deign to look at our petitions? Does it not appear, as clear as the sun... that there is a regular, systematic plan formed to fix the right and practice of taxation upon us? Does not the uniform conduct of Parliament for some years past confirm this...Is there any thing to be expected from petitioning after this? Is not the attack upon the liberty and property of the people of Boston...plain and self-evident proof of what they are aiming at? Do not the subsequent bills...for depriving Massachusetts of its charter...convince us that the administration is determined to stick at nothing to carry its point? Ought we not, then, to put our virtue and fortitude to the severest test? With you I think it a folly to attempt more than we can execute...yet I think we may do more than is generally believed, in respect to the non-importation scheme.*[23]

---

[22] Ibid.

[23] Runge, "George Washington to Bryan Fairfax, 4 July, 1774," *The Papers of George Washington: Colonial Series, Vol. 10,* 109-110

The freeholders of Fairfax County apparently agreed with Colonel Washington. On July 14th, they met in Alexandria and chose Washington and Charles Broadwater to represent the county at the convention in August.[24] Nicholas Cresswell, a loyal British subject who was stranded in Virginia, commented on the election in his diary:

> *There were three Candidates, the Poll was over in about two hours and conducted with great order and regularity...The Candidates gave the populace a Hogshead of Toddy (what we call punch in England). In the evening the returned Member [Washington] gave a Ball to the Freeholders and Gentlemen of the town. This was conducted with great harmony. Coffee and Chocolate, but no Tea. This Herb is in disgrace amongst them at present.[25]*

The freeholders of Fairfax County followed the election with the passage of resolves that expressed the county's views on the dispute with Great Britain. These resolves, largely written by George Mason, were extensive and bold:

Fairfax County Resolves (Excerpts)   July 17, 1774

> *Our Ancestors, when they left their native Land, and settled in America, brought with them...the Civil-Constitution and Form of Government of the Country they came from; and were by the Laws of Nature and Nations, entitled to all It's Privileges, Immunities and Advantages; which have descended to us their Posterity, and ought of Right to be as fully enjoyed, as if we had still continued within...England.*

---

[24] Rutland, "Fairfax County Resolves, 18 July, 1774," *The Papers of George Mason, Vol. 1,* 209
[25] Nicholas Cresswell, *The Journal of Nicholas Cresswell; 1774-1777,* (New York: The Dial Press, 1924), 27-28

Resolved that the most important and valuable Part of the British Constitution...is the fundamental Principle of the People's being governed by no Laws, to which they have not given their Consent, by Representatives freely chosen by themselves; who are affected by the Laws they enact equally with their Constituents; to whom they are accountable...for if this Part of the Constitution was taken away, or materially altered, the Government must degenerate either into an absolute and despotic Monarchy, or a tyrannical Aristocracy, and the Freedom of the People be annihilated.

Resolved therefore, as the Inhabitants of the American Colonies are not, and from their Situation can not be represented in the British Parliament, that the legislative Power here can of Right be exercised only by (our) own Provincial Assemblys or Parliaments, subject to the Assent or Negative of the British Crown....

Resolved that the Claim lately assumed and exercised by the British Parliament, of making all such Laws as they think fit, to govern the People of these Colonies, and to extort from us our Money without our Consent, is not only diametrically contrary to the first Principles of the Constitution...but is totally incompatible with the Privileges of a free People, and the natural Rights of Mankind [and] will render our own Legislatures merely nominal and nugatory, and is calculated to reduce us from a State of Freedom and Happiness to Slavery and Misery.

Resolved that Taxation and Representation are in their Nature inseperable; that the Right of withholding, or of giving and granting their own Money is the only effectual Security to a free People, against the Encroachments of Despotisim and Tyranny; and that whenever they yield the One, they must quickly fall Prey to the other...

Resolved that it is our greatest Wish and Inclination, as well as Interest, to continue our Connection with, and Dependence upon the British Government; but tho' we are it's Subjects, we will use every Means which Heaven hath given us to prevent our becoming its Slaves.[26]

Which Course is Best?

Bryan Fairfax believed these forceful resolves were a mistake. He wrote another letter to Washington in mid July and urged restraint. He believed that patient petitions and appeals to Britain had the best chance of changing British policy. Fairfax wanted to wait for the outcome of yet another petition to Parliament before stronger threats and actions were attempted. He maintained that,

Americans ought to consider the Majority of the english Parliament...as acting from honest tho' erroneous principles...Whatever Corruption there may be in the Parliament, whatever unjust designs some Men may have, we ought to gain the Affections of those who mean well; we should strive to conciliate the Affections of [England]...We should have an eye to the next Parliament, and avoid every

---

[26] Rutland, "Fairfax County Resolves, 18 July, 1774," *The Papers of George Mason, Vol. 1,* 201- 204

measure that might justly exasperate the People. It is incredible how far a mild Behavior contributes to a Reconciliation in any dispute between Man & Man....[27]

Fairfax reasserted his fear that an aggressive approach towards Parliament would only offend and anger that body and insure the rejection of colonial appeals:

For these Reasons I ardently wish that no Resolves had been entered into...No Conditional Resolutions should be published until it is known that the Petition has had no Effect...To petition and to threaten at the same time seems to be inconsistent....[28]

Colonel Washington had already abandoned hope that the petitions would sway Parliament. He responded to Fairfax on July 20th and exclaimed that

I see nothing to induce a belief that the Parliament would embrace a favorable opportunity of repealing acts, which they go on with great rapidity to pass, in order to enforce their tyrannical system; [In fact], *I observe...that* [parliament] *is pursuing a regular plan at the expense of law and justice to overthrow our constitutional rights and liberties. How can I expect any redress from a measure,* [petition] *which has been ineffectually tried already? For, Sir, what is it we are contending against? Is it against paying the duty of three pence per pound on tea because* [it is] *burthensome? No, it is the right only, we have all along disputed, and to this end we have already*

---

[27] Runge, "Bryan Fairfax to George Washington, 17 July, 1774," *The Papers of George Washington, Vol. 10,* 115-116
[28] Ibid.

petitioned his Majesty in as humble and dutiful manner as subjects could do. Nay, more, we applied to [Parliament] *setting forth, that, as Englishmen, we could not be deprived of* [our constitutional rights].[29]

Washington maintained that Parliament's harsh treatment of Massachusetts demonstrated its intention to force arbitrary rule over the colonies. He noted that,

The conduct of the Boston people could not justify the rigor of [parliament's] *measures...has not General Gage's conduct since his arrival* [in Boston]...*exhibited the most despotic system of tyranny, that ever was practised in a free government? In short, what further proofs are wanted to* [confirm] *the designs of the ministry...to fix the right of taxation? What hope then from petitioning? Shall we, after this, whine and cry for relief, when we have already tried it in vain? Or shall we supinely sit and see one province after another fall prey to despotism? If I was in any doubt, as to the right which the Parliament of Great Britain had to tax us without our consent, I should most heartily* [agree] *with you in opinion, that to petition, and petition only, is the proper method to apply for relief...but no such* [doubt do] *I have.*[30]

Washington then summed up the dispute in simple terms.

---

[29] Runge, "George Washington to Bryan Fairfax, 20 July, 1774," *The Papers of George Washington, Vol. 10,* 129
[30] Ibid.

I think the Parliament of Great Britain hath no more right to put their hands into my pocket, without my consent, than I have to put my hands into yours for money; and this being already urged to them in a firm, but decent manner, by all the colonies, what reason is there to expect any thing from their justice?[31]

Washington followed this letter with another in August that re-iterated what was at stake. He believed that unless the colonists defended their rights, they would soon be reduced to a state of servitude to England.

I could wish, I own, that the dispute had been left to posterity to determine, but the crisis is arrived when we must assert our rights, or submit to every imposition, that can be heaped upon us, till custom and use shall make us as tame and abject slaves, as the blacks we rule over with such arbitrary sway.[32]

The Virginia Convention & Continental Congress

The First Virginia Convention met in Williamsburg in early August. Governor Dunmore was out of town, leading a military expedition against the Indians on the frontier, and most of the delegates held similar views on the dispute with Britain, so there was little controversy. Many of the representatives, including George Washington and Charles Broadwater of Fairfax County, Francis Peyton and Thompson Mason of Loudoun County, and Henry Lee II and Thomas Blackburn of Prince William County, arrived with instructions

---

[31] Ibid.
[32] Runge, "George Washington to Bryan Fairfax, 24 August, 1774," *The Papers of George Washington, Vol. 10,* 155

from their county and town committees that called for bold action. They met in the capitol and unanimously voted to send delegates to Philadelphia for a general congress in September. The Convention sent Peyton Randolph, George Washington, Patrick Henry, Richard Henry Lee, Edmund Pendleton, Benjamin Harrison, and Richard Bland to the Congress with instructions to reaffirm Virginia's desire for close ties with Britain. They were also told to defend the colonists' constitutional rights:

> *We desire that they* [the delegates to Congress] *will express...our Faith and true Allegiance to his Majesty King George the Third...and that we are determined...to support him in the legal Exercise of all his just Rights and Prerogatives...We sincerely...wish most ardently a Return of that... Affection and commercial Connexion that formerly united both Countries, which can only be effected by a Removal of those Causes of Discontent* [the Intolerable Acts] *which have of late unhappily divided us. It cannot admit of a Doubt but that British Subjects in America are entitled to the same Rights and Privileges as their Fellow Subjects posses in Britain; and therefore, that the Power assumed by the British Parliament to bind America by their* [laws] *in all Cases whatsoever, is unconstitutional, and the Source of these unhappy Differences.*[33]

The Virginia Convention endorsed a boycott of most British goods to begin on November 1st, 1774, unless Parliament repealed its acts against Massachusetts. Other provisions called for a ban on the importation of slaves and a

---

[33] Van Schreeven and Scribner, "The Convention of 1774: Instructions to the Deputies Elected to Attend the General Congress, 6 August, 1774," *Revolutionary Virginia, Vol. 1,* 236-238

ban on the consumption of tea. The Convention even went as far as to authorize a ban on colonial exports to Britain, to begin in August 1775, if Parliament remained intransigent with its policies.[34]

Virginia's delegates joined the first Continental Congress in Philadelphia in the fall of 1774. Although Massachusetts had been at the center of the dispute with Britain, the delegates chose Peyton Randolph, Virginia's Speaker of the House of Burgesses, to preside over the Congress. The proposals endorsed by the Virginia Convention were largely adopted in October. A boycott of British goods and the discontinuation of the slave trade were approved for December 1st, 1774. A ban on all exports to Britain would follow on September 1st, 1775. Congress also called on the American colonists to be more frugal and industrious, and to avoid extravagant activities like horse-racing, gambling, plays, and dances. Committees were authorized in every county, city, and town to enforce these provisions.[35]

Independent Militia Companies

Most of Virginia's counties had already formed committees over the summer. Some went further and formed their own independent militia companies. Fairfax County was the first to do this. On September 21st, 1774, George Mason chaired a meeting of county freeholders in Alexandria that resulted in the formation of the Fairfax County Militia Association. The meeting proclaimed that,

---

[34] Ibid.
[35] Journal of Continental Congress, 20 October, 1774, 75-80
(Accessed via the Library of Congress website at www.loc.gov)

*In this Time of extreme Danger, with the Indian
Enemy in our Country, and threat'ned with the
Destruction of our Civil-rights, & Liberty, and all
that is dear to British Subjects & Freemen; we the
Subscribers, taking into consideration the present
alarming Situation of all the British Colonies upon
this Continent [and] being sensible of the Expediency
of putting the Militia...upon a more respectable
Footing, & hoping to excite others by our Example,
have voluntarily, freely & cordially entered into the
following Association; which we...solemnly promise,
& pledge our Honours to each other, and to our
Country to perform.*[36]

The company was called the Fairfax Independent Company of
Volunteers and consisted of one hundred men. The members
agreed to

*Meet at such Times & Places in this County as our
Officers (to be chosen by a Majority of the Members)
shall appoint & direct, for the Purpose of learning &
practicing the military Exercise & Discipline.*[37]

Their uniform was, "*a regular Uniform of Blue, turn'd up with
Buff; with plain yellow metal Buttons, Buff Waist Coat &
Breeches, & white Stockings.*"[38] The men were expected to
furnish themselves with " *a good Fire-lock & Bayonet, Sling
Cartouch-Box, and Tomahawk,*" as well as, "*six pounds of
Gunpowder, twenty pounds of Lead, and fifty Gun-flints, at the
least.*"[39]

---

[36] Rutland, "Fairfax County Militia Association, 21 September, 1774," *The
Papers of George Mason, Vol. 1,* 210-211
[37] Ibid.
[38] Ibid.
[39] Ibid

George Washington, who was still in Philadelphia with the Continental Congress, was chosen to lead the company. He received a letter in October asking him to obtain fifes, drums, a flag, and other military supplies.[40] While Washington worked to fulfill the request, the company held military drills in Alexandria. Such exercises added to the militaristic atmosphere of northern Virginia. Nicholas Cresswell complained in his diary on October 24th, that,

> *Everything here [Alexandria] is in the utmost confusion. Committees are appointed to inspect into the Characters and Conduct of every tradesman, to prevent them selling Tea or buying British Manufactures. Some of them have been tarred and feathered, others had their property burnt and destroyed by the populace. Independent Companies are raising in every County on the Continent...and train their Men as if they were on the Eve of War...[Contributions are raised] in every Colony on the Continent for the relief of the people of Boston. The King is openly cursed, and his authority set at defiance. In short, everything is ripe for rebellion. The New Englanders by their canting, whining, insinuating tricks have persuaded the rest of the Colonies that the Government is going to make absolute slaves of them.[41]*

A week later Cresswell heard the resolves of the First Continental Congress read to a crowd in Alexandria. He was not pleased:

---

[40] Runge, "Fairfax Independent Company to George Washington, 19 October, 1774," *The Papers of George Washington: Colonial Series, Vol. 10,* 173

[41] Cresswell Journal, 24 October, 1774, 43-44

This evening went to the Tavern to hear the Resolves of the Continental Congress. Read a Petition to the Throne and an address to the people of Great Britain. Both of them full of duplicity and false representation. I look upon them as insults to the understanding and dignity of the British Sovereign and people...I am sorry to see them so well received by the people and the sentiments so universally adopted. It is a plain proof that the seeds of rebellion are already sown and have taken very deep root, but am in hopes they will be eradicated next summer.[42]

On November 3rd, Cresswell watched the Fairfax Independent Company exercise and shoot an effigy of the British Prime Minister, Lord North.[43] Six weeks later, Cresswell observed independent militia company of Loudoun County drill. He was not impressed and described them as "*a ragged crew*".[44]

Prince William County formed its own independent militia company in November. On November 11th, 1774, the company asked Colonel George Washington to take command of the unit:

Resolved unanimously that Thomas Blackburn, Richard Graham, and Philip Richard Francis Lee Gentlemen, do wait upon Collonel George Washington, and request of him to take the command of this Company as their Field Officer, and that he will be pleas'd to direct the fashion of their uniform; That they also acquaint him with the Motto of the

---

[42] Ibid., 1 November, 1774, 45-46
[43] Ibid., 3 November, 1774, 46
[44] Ibid., 13 December, 1774, 51

Company [Aut liber, aut nullus: Either Liberty or Death] *which is to be fixed on their Colours.*[45]

In late December, one of Prince William County's leaders, William Grayson, wrote to Washington at Mount Vernon and requested that he help the company acquire needed supplies:

> *The gentlemen of the Company...will be much oblig'd to you, to write to Philada for forty muskets with bayonets, Cartouch boxes, or Pouches, and slings, to be made in such a manner, as you shall think proper to direct.*[46]

Washington contacted William Milnor in Philadelphia to obtain the items. On January 3rd, 1775, Milnor wrote to Washington to update his progress:

> *I engaged 40 Musquets this Morning, Mr. Palmer says he will Certainly have them all ready by the first of April, the Cartouch boxes, I have agreed for, at a Dollar each – I intend having one Musquet & one Cartouch box finished & put on board* [with] *Capt. Cobourn, who is now ready to sail...the Drums,* [colors] *& fifes are already on board.*[47]

Similar arrangements were made for many other militia companies in Virginia. They were all preparing for war, and the residents of Fairfax, Loudoun, and Prince William County led the way.

---

[45] Stanislaus M. Hamilton, ed., "Extracts from the Minutes of the Independent Company of Cadets of the 11th November, 1774," *Letters to Washington & Accompanying Papers, Vol. 5*, (Boston & New York: Houghton, Mifflin, Co., 1902), 68-69

[46] Runge, "William Grayson to George Washington, 27 December, 1774," *The Papers of George Washington: Colonial Series, Vol. 10*, 214-215

[47] Runge, "William Milnor to George Washington, 3 January, 1775," *The Papers of George Washington: Colonial Series, Vol. 10*, 224

Chapter Three

"Nothing But War Talked Of..."
1775

No county in Virginia surpassed Fairfax in military preparedness. It was the first to form an independent militia company in 1774, and one of the first to expand its militia in 1775. On January 17th, 1775, the Fairfax Committee of Safety urged that additional militia companies be formed in the county:

> *As well regulated militia, composed of gentlemen, freeholders, and other freemen, is the natural strength and only staple security of a free government...it is recommended to* [the]...*inhabitants of this county* [between] *sixteen to fifty years of age, to form themselves into companies of 68 men...They* [should] *provide themselves with good firelocks, and use their utmost endeavours to make themselves masters of the military exercise published by order of his majesty in 1764.*[1]

The committee explained this action as an attempt to

> *Relieve our mother country from any expense in our protection and defence...*[eliminate] *the...necessity for taxing us...and render it unnecessary to keep standing armies among us.*[2]

---

[1] Rutland, "Fairfax County Committee of Safety Proceedings, 17 January, 1775," *The Papers of George Mason, Vol. 1,* 212
[2] Ibid.

A three shilling tax on every tithable person (all males -- free or slave -- over sixteen as well as female slaves over sixteen) in the county was adopted to pay for the troops.[3]

Three weeks later, George Mason introduced a more specific plan of defense for Fairfax County:

> *Firmly determined, at the hazard of our Lives, to transmit to our Children & Posterity those sacred Rights to which ourselves were born...WE the Subscribers, Inhabitants of Fairfax County, have freely & voluntarily agreed...to enroll & embody ourselves into a Militia for this County, intended to consist of all the able-bodied Freemen from eighteen to fifty Years of Age...[They are to form themselves] into distinct Companies of Sixty-eight Men each...Keep a good Fire-lock in proper Order, and furnish [themselves]...with one pound of Gun Powder, four pounds of Lead, one Dozen Gun-Flints & a pair of Bullet Molds, with a Cartouch Box, or powder horn, and bag for balls.[4]*

Mason proposed that those who had rifles, instead of muskets, form a special company:

> *Such of us have, or can procure Riphel Guns, & understand the use of them, will be ready to form a Company of Marksmen or Light-Infantry... distinguishing [their] Dress, when upon Duty, from that of the other Companies, by painted Hunting Shirts and Indian Boots, or Caps....[5]*

---

[3] Ibid.

[4] Rutland, "Fairfax County Militia Plan for Embodying the People, 6 February, 1775," *The Papers of George Mason, Vol. 1,* 215-216

[5] Ibid.

Mason sent a copy of his plan to Colonel Washington, who was busy supervising the original Fairfax and Prince William independent militia companies.

Washington was also involved in efforts to obtain more military supplies. Muskets, cartouch boxes, sashes, drums, and books on military drill were some of the items procured.[6] These acquisitions enhanced the appearance and conduct of the independent companies. On March 18th, 1775, Nicholas Cresswell, no fan of the militia, observed the Fairfax County militia exercise in Alexandria and noted in his diary that,

> *The Gentlemen and Mechanic Independent Companies* [were] *reviewed by Col. George Washington. All of them in uniform. The Gentlemen, blue and buff. The Mechanics red and blue. In all about 150 men and make a formidable appearance.*[7]

Second Virginia Convention

Colonel Washington did not linger in Alexandria after the troop review. The 2nd Virginia Convention convened in Richmond on March 20th, and Washington joined Charles Broadwater, Henry Lee II, Thomas Blackburn and Francis Peyton to represent the northern counties of Virginia.[8]

The first few days of the Convention were rather uneventful, highlighted by a resolution of thanks to the congressional delegates for their service in Philadelphia. The most important issue of the meeting was introduced on March 23rd. On that day, the delegates considered Patrick Henry's proposal that the "*Colony be immediately put into a posture of*

---

[6] Runge, "William Milnor to George Washington, 3 January, 1775 and 21 February, 1775," *The Papers of George Washington: Colonial Series, Vol. 10,* 224 and 270

[7] Cresswell Journal, 18 March, 1775 58-59

[8] William J. Van Schreeven and Robert L. Scribner, *Revolutionary Virginia: The Road to Independence, Vol. 2* (University Press of Virginia, 1975), 337

defense."[9] Henry called for a committee to *"prepare a Plan for embodying, arming and disciplining such a Number of Men as may be sufficient for that purpose."*[10] Debate on the proposals was intense and culminated with Patrick Henry's famous plea to "Give Me Liberty or Give Me Death." His appeal worked, and the resolution passed by a narrow margin.

A committee was formed to create a detailed plan of defense for Virginia. It included George Washington, Patrick Henry, Richard Henry Lee, Edmund Pendleton, and Thomas Jefferson.[11] They presented their plan to the Convention on March 25th. It called on the counties to form militia companies of 68 men each and to provide every man with

> *A good Rifle if to be had, or otherwise with a Common Firelock, Bayonet and Cartouch Box; and also with a Tomahawk, one pound of Gunpowder, and four pounds of Ball...that* [the men] *be cloathed in a hunting Shirt by Way of Uniform; and that all endeavour as soon as possible to become acquainted with the military Exercise for Infantry appointed by...his Majesty in...1764.*[12]

Given the debate on Henry's initial proposal to assume a posture of defense, the committee's action was rather timid. In fact, many of the counties, including Fairfax and Prince William, had formed such militia companies months earlier so the committee's action did little to increase Virginia's troop strength. The plan merely legitimized the existence of these militia companies.

The other important item of business of the Convention was the selection of delegates to the Second Continental Congress in May. With little debate, the Convention returned

---

[9] Ibid., 366-367
[10] Ibid.
[11] Ibid., 376
[12] Ibid., 375

the seven delegates who attended the first Congress and then adjourned.

The weeks following the convention was surprisingly calm. Colonel Washington and the other delegates to the 2nd Continental Congress prepared to leave for Philadelphia, and their fellow Virginians prepared their fields for spring planting.

The Gunpowder Incident

The calm was broken in the early morning hours of April 21st. Governor Dunmore, concerned with the actions of the convention, quietly transferred a large supply of the colony's gunpowder from the powder magazine in Williamsburg to a British ship in the James River. British marines were observed loading the powder, and an alarm quickly spread through town. By the time a crowd gathered at the courthouse, which was across the street from the powder magazine, the marines were on their way to the James River. Some of the townspeople proposed that they march to the Governor's residence to confront Lord Dunmore. Others went further and suggested that the governor be seized.[13]

Williamsburg's town fathers eventually calmed the crowd and drew up a petition to the governor. The town mayor, John Dixon, and the town aldermen led the crowd to Dunmore's residence to deliver the petition. The Governor informed the gathering that he moved the gunpowder to a more secure place to protect the colony from a possible slave uprising. He claimed that if the powder was needed it would be available within a half hour of the request. For the time being, however, the powder would stay aboard a British ship. Williamsburg's leaders surprisingly accepted this explanation and convinced

---

[13] Ivor Noel Hume, *1775: Another Part of the Field*, (New York: Alfred A. Knopf, 1966), 140

the crowd to do likewise.[14] The crisis was averted, at least temporarily.

The northern counties of Virginia were not as easily placated. When news of the gunpowder incident reached Fredericksburg and the surrounding area, county committees scrambled to organize their militia companies. Officers from the Prince William company wrote to their commander Colonel Washington on April 26th, and informed him that the company had unanimously voted to march to Williamsburg.[15]

Hundreds of armed men gathered in Fredericksburg to march on the capital. Before they departed, however, messengers were sent to Williamsburg to obtain the latest information. They reached Williamsburg in twenty-four hours and discovered a calm capital. Peyton Randolph and other local leaders informed the messengers that troops were not needed, and their arrival would actually complicate matters. The riders returned to Fredericksburg with a letter from Randolph that expressed his appreciation to the volunteers and assured them that the situation was under control:

> *His Excellency* [Dunmore] *has repeatedly assured several Respectable Gentlemen that his only motive in Removing the Powder was to secure it....* [Dunmore] *has given private assurances to Several Gentlemen that the Powder shall be Return'd to the Magazine...It is our opinion and most eanest request that Matters may be quieted for the present;* [We feel the arrival of troops in Williamsburg] *may produce effects, which God only knows the consequence of.*[16]

---

[14] Ibid., 142

[15] Hamilton, "The Independent Company of Prince William to George Washington, 26 April, 1775," *Letters to Washington & Accompanying Papers, Vol. 5*, 163-164

[16] Robert L. Scribner and Brent Tarter, *Revolutionary Virginia: The Road to Independence, Vol. 3*, (University Press of Virginia, 1977), 64

Randolph's moderation helped restore calm in Virginia and most of the militia returned to their homes. Patrick Henry was an exception. He gathered over 150 men (some reports claimed upwards of 500 men) in Hanover County to march on Williamsburg.[17] When Williamsburg's leaders informed Henry that his presence in the capital was not needed, Henry shifted his attention to the Receiver General (the chief tax collector) of the colony, Richard Corbin. Henry sent men to Corbin's house in King and Queen County to demand payment for the stolen gunpowder. If payment was not forthcoming, the men were ordered to seize Corbin. Neither Corbin, nor the money, was at his house, so the party returned empty handed.[18]

The threat that Henry and his men posed to Dunmore's authority forced the Governor to offer payment for the powder. This appeased Henry, and he declared the affair closed and sent his men home.[19] Governor Dunmore, however, was angered by Henry's actions. He viewed them as an affront and proclaimed on May 6th,

> *Whereas...Patrick Henry...and a Number of deluded Followers have taken up Arms* [and] *have...put themselves in a Posture of War...exciting the People to join in these outrageous and rebellious Practices...in open Defiance of Law and Government...I have thought proper...to issue this Proclamation strictly charging all persons, upon their Allegiance, not to aid, abet, or give Countenance to, the said Patrick Henry...but on the contrary, to oppose* [him]*...by every means.*[20]

---

[17] Hume, 169

[18] Ibid., 168

[19] Ibid., 172

[20] Scribner and Tarter, *Revolutionary Virginia: The Road to Independence, Vol. 3,* 101

Henry, who was on his way to Philadelphia to attend the 2nd Continental Congress, was not troubled by the proclamation. Many Virginians, however, were concerned for Henry's safety and rallied to his defense. On May 22nd, the Prince William County Committee unanimously agreed that,

> *The thanks of this committee are justly due to captain Patrick Henry, and the Gentlemen Volunteers who attended him, for their proper and spirited conduct on* [the recent] *alarming occasion.*[21]

Loudoun County was even more direct in its praise for Henry:

> *Resolved, that we cordially approve the conduct of our countrymen, captain Patrick Henry, and the other volunteers of Hanover county, who marched under him, in making reprisals of the king's property for the trespass committed* [taking the gunpowder].[22]

The Continental Army

Although the crisis in Virginia temporarily abated, events in the north were anything but calm. Thousands of New England troops surrounded the King's army in Boston, ready to resume a fight that erupted at Lexington and Concord on April 19th. In early June, the Continental Congress received a request from Joseph Warren, the President of the Provisional Convention of Massachusetts, to assume authority over the army outside of Boston:

---

[21] Ibid., 160
[22] Ibid., 171-172

> *As the army now collecting from different colonies is*
> *for the general defence of the rights of America, we*
> *Beg leave to suggest to* [your] *consideration the*
> *propriety of* [your] *taking the regulation and general*
> *direction of it....* [23]

On June 14th, Congress granted Warren's request and assumed authority over the army. It also authorized the formation of ten rifle companies for the new American army.[24] Virginia raised two of the companies, commanded by Captains Daniel Morgan and Hugh Stephenson. The next day, Congress unanimously chose George Washington as commander of the continental forces. Washington was awed by the responsibility and replied to Congress on June 16th:

> *Tho' I am truly sensible of the high Honour done me*
> *in the Appointment, yet I feel a great distress, from a*
> *consciousness that my abilities & Military experience*
> *may not be equal to the extensive & important Trust:*
> *However, as the Congress desire it I will enter upon*
> *the momentous duty, & exert every power I Possess*
> *In their service & for the Support of the glorious*
> *Cause.* [25]

Prior to his departure to Boston, Washington wrote to the officers of the Virginia militia companies under his command:

---

[23] Journals of the Continental Congress, 2 June, 1775
[24] Ibid., 14 June, 1775
[25] Philander D. Chase, "Address to the Continental Congress, 16 June, 1775," *The Papers of George Washington: Revolutionary War Series, Vol. 1,* 1

I am now about to bid adieu to the Companies under your respective commands, at least for awhile – I have launched into a wide & extensive field, too boundless for my abilities, & far, very far beyond my experience – I am called by the unanimous voice of the Colonies to the command of the Continental army: an honour I did not aspire to – an honour I was solicitous to avoid upon full conviction of my inadequacy...I shall tomorrow, set out for [Boston]. [26]

Washington urged the officers to continue training their men.

The officers of Fairfax County's independent militia responded to Washington's letter in mid July. They wrote that while they deplored

The unfortunate occasion, that calls you, their patron, friend, & worthy citizen from them... they beg your acceptance of their most hearty congratulations upon your appointment.... [27]

The officers expressed their confidence in Washington and assured him that they would continue to train the militia. They also pledged to join Washington in Boston the moment he called for their assistance:

Firmly convinced Sir, of your zealous attachment to the rights of your Country & those of mankind, and of your earnest desire that harmony & Good will should again take place between us & our parent state, we well know that your every exertion will be invariably employed, to preserve the one & effect the other.

---

[26] Chase, "General Washington to John Augustine Washington, 20 June, 1775," *The Papers of George Washington, Vol. 1,* 19

[27] Chase, "The Fairfax Independent Company to General Washington, 8 July, 1775," *The Papers of George Washington, Vol. 1,* 77

Your kind recommendation, that a strict attention be had, to disciplining the Company, shall be complied with...We are to inform you Sir, by desire of the Company, that if at any time you shall judge it expedient for them to join the Troops at Cambridge, or to march elsewhere, they will cheerfully do it.[28]

Third Virginia Convention

Despite this willingness to support their fellow Virginian, a year passed before the colony sent men north to join Washington. The delay was largely caused by Virginia's own military concerns. In June, relations between Lord Dunmore and the House of Burgesses deteriorated to the point that Dunmore and his family fled the capital for the safety of a British warship. The Burgesses were baffled by Dunmore's actions and urged the governor to return to Williamsburg. He refused, and the stalemate threw the colony in political limbo.

In mid-July, the 3rd Virginia Convention met in Richmond and partially filled the political void. Prince William County once again sent Henry Lee II and Thomas Blackburn as delegates. Loudoun County sent Francis Peyton and Josias Clapham, and Fairfax County sent George Mason and Charles Broadwater.[29] Lee, Blackburn, and Mason served on the most important committee of the convention, one that sought to raise *"a sufficient armed Force...for the Defence and protection of this Colony."* [30]

A week into the committee's deliberation, a tired George Mason wrote home and outlined the enormous challenge before the committee:

---

[28] Ibid.
[29] Scribner & Tarter, *Revolutionary Virginia, Vol. 3,* 305-306
[30] Ibid., 319

*I have not...had an hour which I could call my own.
The committee... meets every morning at seven o'
clock, sits till the Convention meets, which seldom
[ends] before five in the afternoon, and immediately
after dinner and a little refreshment sits again till
nine or ten at night. This is hard duty, and yet, we
have hitherto made but little progress....This will not
be wondered at when the extent and importance of
the business before us is reflected on – to raise forces
for immediate service – to new model the whole
militia – to render about one-fifth of it fit for the field
at the shortest warning – to melt down all the
volunteer and independent companies into this great
establishment – to provide arms, ammunition, &c., --
and to point out ways and means of raising money,
these are difficulties indeed!* [31]

By mid-August the committee overcame these difficulties and
submitted its plan for the convention's approval.

Virginia's New Military

The committee's plan significantly enhanced Virginia's
military capabilities. All of the independent militia companies
were dissolved and replaced by a three tiered military system.
The top tier consisted of two regiments of regular (full time)
soldiers who enlisted for one year. The 1st Virginia Regiment
totaled 544 men (not including the officers) and was divided
into eight companies of sixty-eight men. [32] Patrick Henry was
selected by the convention to command the regiment.[33] The
2nd Virginia consisted of seven companies and totaled 476

---

[31] Rutland, "George Mason to Martin Cockburn, 24 July, 1775," *The
Papers of George Mason, Vol. 1,* 241
[32] William W. Hening, *The Statutes at Large Being a Collection of all the
Laws of Virginia, Vol. 9,* (Richmond: J. & G. Cochran, 1821), 9
[33] Scribner and Tartar, Vol. 3, 400

men.[34]   Colonel William Woodford of Caroline County
commanded this regiment. [35]

For recruitment purposes the Convention organized
Virginia into sixteen districts and ordered each district to raise
a company of regular troops.[36] Prince William, Fairfax, and
Loudoun County formed one district and recruited a company
of men under Captain George Johnston of Loudoun County.
Johnston was a member of the Loudoun County Committee of
Correspondence and helped pass the Loudoun County
Resolves in June 1774. He was destined to see combat at
Great Bridge, rise to the rank of lieutenant colonel, and serve
as an aide to General Washington in 1777. Sadly, after only
six months of service to Washington, Johnston succumbed to
an illness and died.[37]

In 1775, however, Johnston was healthy, and his company
was formed in a matter of weeks. Captain Johnston and his
men arrived in Williamsburg in late September and were
attached to Colonel William Woodford's 2nd Virginia
Regiment. They spent the next few weeks training and
outfitting themselves with hunting shirts and military
accoutrements.[38]

The regular troops were not the only soldiers in
Williamsburg. Hundreds of minutemen arrived in the fall to
bolster the capital's defense. They comprised the second tier
of Virginia's new military establishment. The 3rd Virginia
Convention authorized sixteen battalions of minutemen.
These men were drawn from the ranks of the militia and were
"more strictly trained to proper discipline" [than the ordinary

---

[34] Hening, Vol. 9, 10,
[35] Scribner and Tartar, Vol. 3, 457-458
[36] Hening, Vol. 9, 10, 16
[37] Chase, "General Orders, 20 January, 1777," *The Papers of George Washington, Vol. 8,* 111
[38] Mary Godwin, *Cloathing and Accoutrements of the Officers and Soldiers of the Virginia Forces: 1775-1788,* (Unpublished, 1962), 21, 43-46

militia.[39]   Each district was ordered to raise a 500 man battalion of minutemen *"from the age of sixteen to fifty, to be divided into ten companies of fifty men each."* [40]   Like the regular troops, the minutemen were provided with proper arms as well as a hunting shirt and leggings.[41]

Once the minute battalions raised the necessary men, they were mustered and trained for twenty straight days. Following this, the companies of each minute battalion were expected to exercise every month for four days. Additionally, after the twenty day drill, each battalion assembled for twelve day training sessions twice a year. The battalion of minutemen raised from Prince William, Fairfax, and Loudoun counties was designated the Prince William Battalion and was ordered to muster for their twelve day drills in mid May and late October.[42]

The battalion was commanded by Colonel William Grayson of Prince William. Grayson was a prominent resident of Dumfries and one of Prince William County's most important leaders.   He was a member of the County Committee of Correspondence and one of the chief organizers of the county's original independent militia company.

John Quarles, of Prince William, was appointed lieutenant colonel and Levin Powell, of Loudoun County, was named the battalion's major.[43] Like many officers, Powell was an active member of his county's committee of correspondence before his appointment to the battalion.

It is unclear whether the battalion reached its authorized strength of 500 men.   Only six companies have been identified. Prince William contributed three, commanded by captains Cuthbert Harrison, Philip Richard Francis Lee, and

---

[39] Hening, Vol. 9, 16

[40] Ibid., 16-17

[41] Ibid., 20

[42] Ibid., 20-21

[43] Scribner and Tarter, *Revolutionary Virginia: The Road to Independence,* *Vol. 6,* 75, 230, 235

Andrew Leitch. Loudoun County raised two under Simon Triplett and Charles West, and Captain John Fitzgerald led the company of Fairfax County minutemen. The battalion remained in northern Virginia until December 1775, when it was ordered to Williamsburg.

The last tier of Virginia's new military establishment was the traditional county militia. The Convention decreed that:

> *All male persons, hired servants, and apprentices, above the age of sixteen, and under fifty years...shall be enlisted into the militia...and formed into companies....*[44]

Each member of the county militia had six months to furnish himself with

> *A good rifle...with a tomahawk,* [or a] *common firelock, bayonet, pouch, or cartouch box, three charges of powder and ball....* [Members of the militia] *shall constantly keep by him one pound of powder and four pounds of ball....*[45]

The militia companies were ordered to hold private musters every two weeks, except in December, January, and February.

---

[44] Hening, 27-28
[45] Ibid.

War Fever

The military spirit that gripped Virginia in 1775 convinced Lund Washington, a relative of George Washington and the caretaker of Mount Vernon in the general's absence, that Virginia could adequately defend itself. On September 29th, 1775, he updated General Washington on Fairfax County's success in recruiting men for military service:

> *Our Committee has made Choice of their Militia officers. Colo. [Charles] West [is the County] Lieutenant, McCarty & Broadwater [are colonels and], Robt. Harrison [is appointed major]. The Captns, Lieutenants & Ensigns are dispers'd in different parts of the [county] a great many of them...are of our [independent] Company, 40 I believe altogether for the Minute Service & Militia.*[46]

The formation of these units relieved some of the anxiety Lund Washington and others had about Mrs. Washington's safety. Many northern Virginians were concerned that Lord Dunmore planned to raid Mount Vernon. Gentlemen from as far as Loudoun County offered to escort Mrs. Washington to the interior of the colony. Lund Washington wrote to General Washington in early October to assure the general that his wife was safe and a move inland was unnecessary:

> *Tis true many people have made a Stir about Mrs Washington's Continuing at Mt. Vernon but I cannot think of her in any Sort of danger – the thought I believed first originated in Alexandria – from thence it got to Loudoun, I am told the people of Loudoun talkd of sendg a Guard to Conduct her to Berkeley*

---

[46] Chase, "Lund Washington to George Washington, 29 September, 1775," *The Papers of George Washington, Vol. 2,* 64-65

with some of their principle men to persuade her to leave Mt Vernon – she does not believe herself in danger, nor do I. [If Dunmore's men] *attempt to take her in the dead of Night they would fail, for 10 minutes notice would be Sufficient for her to go out of the way – Lord Dumore will hardly Venture himself up this River, nor can I think he* [would attempt such a deed], *surely* [Mrs. Washington's] *old acquaintance,* [John Randolph, Virginia's Attorney General], *who with his family are aboard* [Dunmore's] *Ship, would put him off doing an Act of that kind.*[47]

A few weeks later Lund Washington re-iterated his confidence in Mount Vernon's security:

I think 50 men well Arm'd might prevent 200 from burning Mt. Vernon Situated as it is, no way to get to it but up a steep hill…I wish I had the musquets – I would endeavour to find the men Black or White, that would at least make them pay dear for the attempt.[48]

Despite Lund Washington's faith in the local militia and his confidence that Dunmore would not lower himself to the level of a kidnapper, the inhabitants of northern Virginia remained anxious about a possible attack and prepared accordingly. The region, like the rest of the colony, was on a war footing. Loyalist Nicholas Cresswell observed in late October that many residents were moving their valuables inland, away from the Potomac River:

---

[47] Chase, "Lund Washington to George Washington, 5 October, 1775," *The Papers of George Washington, Vol. 2,* 116
[48] Chase, "Lund Washington to George Washington, 29 October, 1775," *The Papers of George Washington, Vol. 2,* 258

October 23rd, 1775

News that Lord Dunmore was coming up the River with four thousand men to destroy the town [Alexandria]…The inhabitants begin to remove their most valuable effects out of town, but I think it will prove a false alarm.[49]

Cresswell also commented on the military activity and public sentiment in Alexandria:

October 20th, 1775

Nothing but War talked of, raising men and making every military preparation. A large army at Boston, another in Canada and another at or about Norfolk in Virginia. This can not be redressing grievances, it is open rebellion and I am convinced if Great Britain does not send more men here and subdue them soon they will declare Independence.

October 30th, 1775

The people here are ripe for a revolt, nothing but curses and imprecations against England, her Fleets, armies, and friends. The King is publicly cursed and rebellion rears her horrid head.[50]

Concern about an attack on northern Virginia proved unwarranted because Lord Dunmore focused his attention and efforts on Norfolk. In mid-November, Dunmore's troops routed a detachment of Princess Ann County militia at Kemps Landing. Dunmore followed the victory with a proclamation that offered freedom to slaves and indentured servants of rebellious Virginians who agreed to fight for him. Hundreds of slaves and servants ran away and joined Dunmore's ranks. Unfortunately for Dunmore, the proclamation alienated a lot

---

[49] Cresswell Journal, 126-127
[50] Ibid.

of moderate Virginians who dumped neutrality and sided with the rebellion. The stage was set for a civil war.

Great Bridge

Lord Dunmore concentrated his forces at Norfolk and worked to secure the town as a base of operation. In late November, he confidently updated General William Howe, the British commander in Boston, on his progress:

> *The inclosed Proclamation...has had a Wonderful effect as there are not less than three thousand that have already taken and signed the inclosed [loyalty] Oath. The Negroes are flocking in also from all quarters which I hope will oblige the Rebels to disperse to take care of their families and property, and had I but a few more men here I would March immediately to Williamsburg my former place of residence by which I should soon compel the whole Colony to Submit.*[51]

Dunmore's bold statement conflicted with his actions, however, for rather than act offensively, Dunmore remained on the defensive. Reports of a large rebel force en route to Norfolk prompted Dunmore to dig in and secure a key river crossing at Great Bridge. He explained his actions to General Howe:

> *Having heard that a thousand chosen Men belonging to the Rebels, a great part of which were Rifle men, were on their March to attack us here so to cut off our provisions, I determined to take possession of the pass at the great Bridge which Secures us the*

---

[51] William Clark, "Dunmore to Major General William Howe, 30 November, 1775," *Naval Documents of the American Revolution, Vol. 2,* 1210

greatest part of two Counties to supply us with provisions. I accordingly ordered a Stockade Fort to be erected there, which was done in a few days, and I put an Officer and Twenty five men to Garrison it, with some Volunteers and Negroes, who have defended it against all efforts of the Rebels for these eight days past, we have killed Several of their Men, and I make no doubt we shall now be able to maintain our ground there, but should we be obliged to abandon it, we have thrown up an Entrenchment on the Land side of Norfolk which I hope they never will be able to force.[52]

The 'chosen men" opposing Dunmore at Great Bridge were elements of the Culpeper Minute Battalion and six companies of the 2nd Virginia Regiment. One of the six companies of regulars was Captain George Johnston's company from northern Virginia. Colonel William Woodford commanded the combined force and spent the early part of December probing Dunmore's defenses. Lord Dunmore described some of these probes in a letter to London:

The Fort has been besieged by between seven or eight hundred of the Rebels for these eight days past, without hitherto doing us the least damage, except wounding one or two Men very Slightly...the Rebels...have made many attempts to Cross the [river] on Rafts, but thank God we have hitherto always repulsed them.[53]

---

[52] Ibid.

[53] Clark, "Dunmore to Lord Dartmouth, 6 December, 1775," *Naval Documents of the American Revolution, Vol. 2,* 1311

With both sides entrenched along opposite sides of the river and the bridge dismantled, the stalemate entered a second week. The situation drastically changed on December 9th, when Lord Dunmore's troops suddenly attacked. Colonel Woodford described how a servant of one of his officers provided Dunmore with false information that caused the Governor to stage an ill advised attack:

> *A servant belonging to major* [Thomas] *Marshal, who deserted the other night from col. Charles Scott's party, has completely taken his lordship in. Lieutenant Batut,* [of Britain's 14th Regiment], *who is wounded, and at present my prisoner, informs, that this fellow told them not more than 300 shirtmen were here; and that* [Dunmore took] *the bait, dispatching capt. Leslie with all the regulars (about 200) who arrived at the bridge about 3 o"clock in the morning, joined* [by] *about 300 black and white slaves, laid planks upon the bridge, and crossed just after our reveille had beat...capt. Fordyce of the grenadiers led the* [attack] *with his company, who, for coolness and bravery, deserved a better fate, as well as the brave fellows who fell with him, who behaved like heroes. They marched up to our breastwork with fixed bayonets, and perhaps a hotter fire never happened, or a greater carnage, for the number of troops.*[54]

A similar account of the attack was given by a British midshipman:

---

[54] Clark, "Colonel William Woodford to Edmund Pendleton, 10 December, 1775," *Naval Documents of the American Revolution, Vol. 3,* 39-40

We marched up to their works with the intrepidity of lions. But, alas! We retreated with much fewer brave fellows than we took out. Their fire was so heavy, that, had we not retreated as we did, we should every one have been cut off. Figure to yourself a strong breast-work built across a causeway, on which six men only could advance a-breast; a large swamp almost surrounding them, at the back of which were two small breast-works to flank us in our attack on their intrenchments. Under these disadvantages it was impossible to succeed; yet our men were so enraged, that all the intreaties, and...threats of their Officers could [not convince] *them to retreat; which at last they did...We had sixty killed, wounded, and taken prisoner....*[55]

The Virginians were thrilled with their victory. Nineteen year old John Marshall, a lieutenant in the Culpeper Minutemen and a future Chief Justice of the Supreme Court, noted that,

Every grenadier is said to have been killed or wounded in this ill-judged attack, while the Americans did not lose a single man.[56]

Colonel Woodford's report was equally upbeat. He declared that the battle *"was a second Bunker's Hill affair, in miniature, with this difference, that we kept our post."*[57]

---

[55] Clark, "Letter from a Midshipman on Board H.M. Sloop Otter, 9 December, 1775," *Naval Documents of the American Revolution, Vol. 3*, 29

[56] John Marshall, *The Life of George Washington, Vol. 2*, (Fredericksburg, VA: The Citizens Guild of Washington's Boyhood Home, 1926), 132

[57] Clark, "Colonel William Woodford to Edmund Pendleton, 10 December, 1775," *Naval Documents of the American Revolution, Vol. 3*, 40

Among the victors were Captain George Johnston and his men from Prince William, Loudoun, and Fairfax Counties.

The "rebel" victory at Great Bridge forced Lord Dunmore to abandon Norfolk and withdraw to the safety of British ships offshore. Although this was a serious setback for Dunmore's efforts to re-establish royal authority in Virginia, his chastised force remained a military threat.

Southeastern Virginia

Chapter Four

"The Sword is Drawn"
1776

The residents of northern Virginia remained anxious at the start of 1776, despite the victory at Great Bridge. With most of the colony's attention and military resources concentrated around Norfolk, northern Virginia felt particularly vulnerable. The Fairfax County Committee urged its delegates at the 4th Virginia Convention to push for more troops to protect the entire colony:

> *We beg you to use your utmost Endeavours, that Men may be rais'd on the Regular Establishment, & Vessells arm'd, to be stationed at such Places as will contribute to the Safety of the Colony at large.* [1]

The Committee was particularly anxious about the security of Alexandria. They complained that the entire upper portion of the colony was undefended:

> *From the present System adopted by those at the Head of Affairs, it wou'd appear that the upper parts of the Colony were to be left destitute of Defence, and totally neglected. Companies on the Minute Service* [are] *call'd out of the Northern District* [while] *those in the Southern one,* [closer] *to the Place for Action have* [not been mustered]. *Why is this part of the Country to be left unguarded when it appears...that Alexandria* [is] *to be* [Dunmore's] *place of rendezvous in the Month of April next.* [2]

---

[1] Rutland, "Instructions of the Fairfax County Committee to Their Delegates, 9 December, 1775," *The Papers of George Mason, Vol. 1*, 261
[2] Ibid.

Lund Washington echoed the committee's concerns in mid January and complained to General Washington that little had been done to defend the region:

> *The Alexandrians expect to have their Town burnt by the Enemy soon – they do not take any steps to prevent it – they put their trust in the Convention... The Minute Battalion is gone to Williamsburg & with them all most all the guns that were worth haveg in the County. Our Militia Exercises with Clubs, if they come to close quarters in an engagement they perhaps may do some Execution but not otherwise....*[3]

Two weeks later Lund Washington reported that people were fleeing the region:

> *Alexandria is much alarm'd, & indeed the whole Neighbourhood – a report prevails that there are five large Ships laying off the mouth of Cane* [Kane's Creek on Mason's Neck] *an express from County to County brings the Information. Altho the River is Block'd up with Ice – the Women & Children are leaveg Alexandria & Stowg themselves into every little Hut they can get, out of the reach of the Enemys Canon...Every Waggon, Cart, & Pack Horse that can be got, are employ'd in moveg the goods out of Town – The Militia are all up (but not in Arms) for Indeed they have none or at least very few.*[4]

---

[3] Philander D. Chase, "Lund Washington to George Washington, 17 January, 1776," *The Papers of George Washington, Vol. 3*, 129-130

[4] Chase, "Lund Washington to George Washington, 31 January, 1776," *The Papers of George Washington, Vol. 3*, 231

The Fairfax Committee appealed to the Convention for more supplies and reminded them that armed conflict was imminent:

The Sword is drawn, the Bayonet is already at our Breasts, therefore some immediate Effort is necessary to ward off the meditated Blow, let the County Lieutenants be supply'd with Arms from the Armory at Fredericksburg, or have Liberty to buy them any where at the Country's Expence.[5]

Despite the anxiety over their weak state of defense, the conflict and tension of 1775 provoked a number of northern Virginians to consider independence from Great Britain. Nicholas Cresswell noted in his diary in January, 1776, that, *"Nothing But Independence*[is] *talked off...The Devil is in the people."*[6] Cresswell blamed a new pamphlet entitled *Common Sense* for some of the dissention:

A pamphlet called Commonsense makes a great noise. One of the vilest things that ever was published to the world. Full of false representations, lies, calumny, and treason, whose principles are to subvert all Kingly Governments and erect an Independent Republic...The sentiments are adopted by a great number of people who are indebted to Great Britain.[7]

Near the end of January, Cresswell was heartened by rumors that Lord Dunmore planned to sail up the Potomac River to Alexandria. Cresswell noted in his journal that, *"I wish his Lordship a safe arrival."*[8]

---

[5] Ibid

[6] Cresswell Journal, "22 and 26 January, 1776," 136

[7] Ibid.

[8] Ibid.

Colonel George Mason hoped otherwise and led an effort to protect Alexandria with a makeshift navy. The challenge he faced was to find enough cannon and supplies to convert civilian vessels into warships. Since Maryland also wished to protect the Potomac River, Mason contacted the Maryland Council of Safety and informed them of his activities:

> *Being employed by the Committee of Safety for this colony to fit out three armed cruisers, & two row gallies, for the protection of* [the] *potomack River, we have...bought three sloops; the largest of which (called the American Congress) will mount 14 Carriage Guns, 6 & 4 pounders, & man'ed with about ninety men. We are now raising the company of Marines, which will be completed in a few days....*[9]

Marines were not the only troops raised in Virginia. The 4th Virginia Convention decided in January 1776 to increase the number of regular regiments from two to nine and double their length of service.[10] Virginia's counties once again stepped up recruitment. By early spring, many of the companies were complete and on their way to rendezvous points.

On February 10th, 1776, the Virginia Committee of Safety eased northern Virginia's anxiety when it ordered Colonel Hugh Mercer's newly created 3rd Virginia Regiment to the region.[11] The selection of the 3rd Regiment made sense because the bulk of the unit was recruited from Fairfax, Prince

---

[9] Scribner and Tarter, "George Mason and John Dalton to the President of the Maryland Council of Safety, 31 January, 1776," *Revolutionary Virginia, Vol. 6,* 40–41

[10] Scribner and Tarter, "Proceedings of the Fourth Virginia Convention, 10 January, 1776," *Revolutionary Virginia, Vol. 5,* 372 and Hening, *Vol. 9,* 81

[11] Scribner and Tarter, "Proceedings of the Fourth Virginia Convention, 10 January, 1776," *Revolutionary Virginia, Vol.6,* 85

William, Loudoun, and the surrounding counties. The company from Fairfax was commanded by Captain John Fitzgerald. Captains Andrew Leitch and Philip Richard Francis Lee commanded companies from Prince William County and Captain Charles West commanded a company of Loudoun County riflemen.[12]

Guarding the Potomac

The 3rd Virginia was originally ordered to Alexandria, but to the chagrin of Lund Washington, it was re-directed to Dumfries, about 25 miles south of Alexandria. Lund informed General Washington about the placement of the 3rd Virginia on February 29th:

> *...The Regiment [3rd Virginia] that...was to be Stationd at Alexandria the Committee of Safety in their great wisdom, has thought fit to order to Dumfries, it being lookd upon as a much properer place, and I suppose much more exposed to danger.*[13]

Lund noted that the residents of Alexandria,

> *Are Buying up Provisions* [and] *bringing down Cannon, from Winchester and other places,* [building] *Vessles etc...but these are trifles and not worth defendg, which I suppose was the Reason why the Regiment did not come here.*[14]

---

[12] E.M. Sanchez-Saavedra, A Guide to Virginia Military Organizations in the American Revolution: 1774-1787, (Westminster, MD: Willow Bend Books, 1978), 39

[13] Chase, "Lund Washington to George Washington, 29 February, 1776, *The Papers of George Washington, Vol. 3*, 396

[14] Ibid.

Elements of the 3rd Virginia arrived in Dumfries in March. Colonel Mercer joined them in the beginning of April. A few weeks earlier, the Committee of Safety assigned Mercer the task of establishing a system of warning beacons along the Potomac River. The Committee contacted Maryland's Council of Safety to solicit its cooperation in the endeavor:

> *The great length of Potomack River from its mouth to Alexandria where* [enemy ships] *can go & the probability of* [an attack] *being made by the Enemy* [along the Potomac River] *make it prudent...to erect beacons or signals for communicating intelligence of their approach up the river in a more speedy manner than can be done by land: We have therefore appointed Colonel Mercer of the third, & Colonel Peachy of the fifth Regiment to Examine the river & fix the different posts & mode of continuing these Signals, but as we are aware that the course of the river will make it necessary that many of them should be set in* [Maryland], *we hope you will approve the measure & name Commissioners on your part to Co-operate with the above named Gentlemen in effecting it.* [15]

Along with the establishment of the beacon system, Mercer was ordered to protect a large stretch of the Potomac River. On April 1st, he wrote to General Charles Lee, the commander of continental forces in the south:

---

[15] Scribner and Tarter, "Edmund Pendleton to Maryland Council of Safety, 9 March, 1776," *Revolutionary Virginia, Vol.6,* 188-89

As soon as Tents can be provided I intend to encamp at Alexandria for the purpose of training the Officers and men, but shall leave a proper guard here [in Dumfries].[15]

The presence of the 3rd Virginia gave some comfort to George Mason. He wrote to General Washington on April 2nd that,

A regiment commanded by Colonel Mercer of Fredericksburg, is stationed on this part of the river, and I hope we shall be tolerably safe, unless a push is made here with a large body of men.[16]

Mason would undoubtedly have been troubled to learn that on the same day he wrote to Washington, General Lee ordered Colonel Mercer to march the 3rd Virginia to Williamsburg:

As there is the greatest reason to conclude...that if the enemy arrive with a considerable force, the possession of Williamsburg and York will be their first object...I think it necessary...to defeat...their design. I must therefore desire that you will march your Regiment to [Williamsburg] without delay.[17]

Poor weather delayed Mercer's march south. On April 10th, he wrote to General Lee from Fredericksburg:

---

[15] " Colonel Hugh Mercer to General Charles Lee, 1 April, 1776," *The Lee Papers, Vol. 1*, (Collections of the New York Historical Society, 1871), 371

[16] Kate Mason Rowland, "George Mason to George Washington, 2 April, 1776," *The Life and Correspondence of George Mason, Vol. 1*, (New York: Russell & Russell, 1964), 219

[17] "General Charles Lee to Colonel Hugh Mercer, 2 April, 1776," *The Lee Papers, Vol. 1*, (Collections of the New York Historical Society, 1871), 369

Northern Virginia

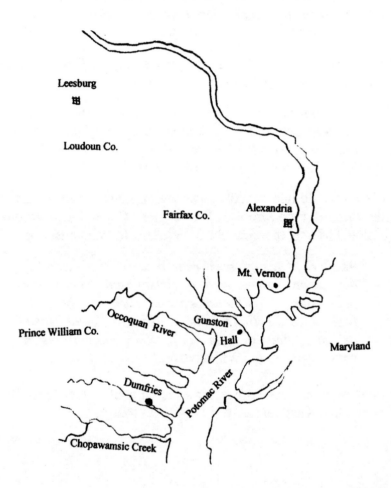

Leesburg

Loudoun Co.

Fairfax Co.

Alexandria

Mt. Vernon

Occoquan River

Gunston
Hall

Prince William Co.

Maryland

Dumfries

Potomac River

Chopawamsic Creek

My Regiment is on the march from Alexandria &
Dumfries, we are much retarded by daily succeeding
Rains, which have render'd the Roads almost
impassable, but will use our utmost endeavour to be
soon at Williamsburg.[18]

The delay was fortunate because, at the prompting of the
Committee of Safety, General Lee reversed his decision. He
ordered Colonel Mercer to return to northern Virginia and
deploy his regiment as he thought best to defend the region:

I must desire that you will remain with your Regiment
for the defence of [northern Virginia and] *as you are*
a much better judge of the manner to station them,
than I can possibly be; for instance, whether the
whole or only a part [should be posted] *at*
Alexandria, I leave [it] *entirely to your good sense*
and discretion.[19]

Colonel Mercer replied to Lee's order on April 14th:

I shall prepare in obedience to your orders...to
resume my former station at Alexandria. That
place... [has] *a considerable quantity of public stores,*
& appears to me to be the principle object, we are to
attend to in defence of the frontier along the
Potowmack River. Guards will also be necessary on
[Occoquan], *Quantico, & Patowmack Creeks. I*
should judge that my Regiment cannot occupy further
along that Frontier without dividing us too much.[20]

---

[18] " Colonel Hugh Mercer to General Charles Lee, 10 April, 1776, *The Lee
Papers, Vol. 1*, 406
[19] "General Charles Lee to Colonel Hugh Mercer, 10 April, 1776, *The Lee
Papers, Vol. 1*, 409
[20] "Col. Hugh Mercer to Gen. Charles Lee," *The Lee Papers, Vol. 1*, 419

Mercer added that, *"We remain very ill provided with arms: the two Companies from Fauquier have not yet joined the Regiment."* [21]

Mercer's regiment remained in northern Virgnina for six weeks. Their stay abruptly ended in late May when Lord Dunmore landed on Gwynn's Island, just off the mainland in Chesapeake Bay. The 3rd Virginia was ordered to Williamsburg as quickly as possible.

Independence

Significant political events occurred in Virginia prior to Dunmore's landing at Gwynn's Island. The growing sentiment for independence that Nicholas Cresswell observed in the winter culminated with the passage of a resolution by the 5th Virginia Convention in favor of independence on May 15th, 1776:

> *Resolved unanimously that the delegates appointed to represent this colony in General Congress be instructed to propose to that respectable body to declare the United Colonies free and independent states absolved from all allegiance to or dependence upon the crown or parliament of Great Britain and that they give the assent of this Colony to such declaration....* [22]

George Mason, one of two Convention delegates from Fairfax County, arrived in Williamsburg a few days after the vote. He immediately wrote to Richard Henry Lee, one of Virginia's delegates in Congress, to inform him of the Convention's action and urge him to return to Virginia to help form a new state government:

---

[21] Ibid.
[22] Scribner and Tarter, "5th VA Convention, 5 May, 1776," *Revolutionary Virginia, Vol. 7 part 1*, 143

We are now going upon the most important of all Subjects – Government: The Committee appointed to prepare a plan is, according to Custom, overcharged with useless members...We shall, in all probability have a thousand ridiculous and impracticable proposals & of Course, a Plan form'd of hetrogenious, jarring & unintelligible Ingredients; this can be prevented only by a few Men of Integrity & Abilitys...I need not tell you how much you will be wanted here on this Occasion...We can not do without you—Mr [Thomas] Nelson is now on his Way to Philadelphia; & will supply your place in Congress....[23]

Despite Mason's high regard for Richard Henry Lee, it was Mason himself who was instrumental in drafting both the Virginia Declaration of Rights and Virginia's first constitution. The Declaration of Rights was introduced to the Virginia Convention on May 27th. It included many ideas that were incorporated in the Declaration of Independence and the Bill of Rights:

That all men are born equally free and independent, and have certain inherent natural rights...among which are, the enjoyment of life and liberty, with the means of acquiring and possessing property, and pursuing and obtaining happiness and safety...

That all power is vested in, and consequently derived from, the people...

That government is, or ought to be, instituted for the common benefit....[24]

---

[23] Rutland, "George Mason to Richard Henry Lee, 18 May, 1776," *The Papers of George Mason, Vol. 1,* 271

[24] Tarter and Scribner, "5th Virginia Convention, 27 May, 1776," *Revolutionary Virginia, Vol. 7 part 2,* 271

Although these lofty sentiments garnered the attention and praise of most Virginians, they were somewhat overshadowed at the time by events on Gwynn's Island.

Gwynn's Island

Lord Dunmore arrived on Gwynn's Island on May 26th and immediately established a fortified position directly across from the mainland. His men enjoyed fresh provisions and the protection of an island that was separated from the mainland by a narrow strip of water.

Troops from the 7th Virginia Regiment and the local militia were the first to respond to Dunmore's landing. Captain Thomas Posey of the 7th Virginia arrived at Gwynn's Island on May 27th and described the scene in his journal:

> *I found a number of the militia assembled, which appear'd to be in the utmost consternation, some running one way, and some another, under no kind of control or regularity.*[25]

Colonel William Daingerfield, the commander of the 7th Virginia, was the highest ranking officer there. He ordered his men, and the militia, to advance closer to the shore to prevent the enemy from landing on the mainland. Posey observed that,

> *The whole were put in motion, (though I must confess the militia were in very great motion before the orders were given). However, these orders served to put them in something grator; for as soon as we came neare enough for the grape[shot], and cannon shot to whistle over our heads, numbers of the militia put*

---

[25] Thomas Posey's Revolutionary War Journal, 27 May, 1776, Thomas Posey Papers, Indiana Historical Society Library, Indianapolis, IN (Referred to henceforth as Posey's Journal)

themselves in much quicker motion, and never stoped...to look behind them until they had made the best of there way home.[26]

Posey was also critical of his own troops:

I cant say that our regulars deserved any great degree of credit for after two or three getting a little blood drawn, they began to skulk and fall flat upon there faces.[27]

Despite their apprehension, Captain Posey and his men held their ground and endured enemy fire and heavy rain all evening. As the hours passed, they grew more determined to face the enemy. Posey recalled,

We began to grow very firm and only wish them to come into the bushes, where we are certain of beating them.[28]

Rather than attack the mainland, however, Lord Dunmore was content to stay on the island and harass the Virginians with artillery fire from his ships. General Andrew Lewis, the commander of Virginia's continental troops, realized that without artillery of his own, his force was powerless to challenge Dunmore. He informed General Charles Lee, the commander of continental troops in the whole south, that he had

Ordered several Pieces of Cannon at Gloucester Town to be mounted which the workmen are about, in order to have them mounted opposite the Enemy and if possible, to prevent some small armed Vessels

---

[26] Ibid.
[27] Ibid.
[28] Posey Journal, 27 May, 1776

getting out which lie between the mainland and the island. I have sent under the Command of Col. Mercer three companies to reinforce Col. Dangerfield's Battalion.... [29]

Colonel Mercer's regiment, the 3rd Virginia, marched to Williamsburg (from northern Virginia) in late May and were held in reserve, while the American forces at Gwynn's Island constructed cannon batteries. The batteries were completed in early July and were revealed to Dunmore in dramatic fashion on the morning of July 9th. Captain Posey described what happened:

Upon the enemies receiving this very unexpected [bombardment], they gave immediate orders to evacuate the Island. On the discovery of which, orders were given to cross into the island and endeavour to harass the enemy in the rear. Col. McClannahan was directed to take command of about 200 men for the afore said purpose. [30]

A lack of boats delayed this crossing until the next morning. By then, Dunmore and his men had evacuated the island and returned to their ships. Captain Posey was one of the first Virginians on Gwynn's Island and described the landing in his diary:

Crossed into the Island but no fighting ensued except a few shot. By one o'clock the whole of the enemy had evacuated and embarked...I cannot help observeing, that I never saw more distress in my life, than what I found among some of the poor deluded Negroes which they could not take time, or did not

---

[29] "General Andrew Lewis to General Charles Lee, 12 June, 1776," *The Lee Papers, Vol. 2,* 63

[30] Posey Journal, 9 July, 1776

chuse to cary off with them, they being sick. Those
that I saw, some were dying, and many calling out for
help; and throughout the whole Island we found them
stre'd about, many of them torn to pieces by wild
beasts – great numbers of the bodies having never
been buried.[31]

British losses at Gwynn's Island are difficult to ascertain.
Captain Posey estimated, *"that at least 4 or 500 negroes lost*
their lives."[32] Posey added that another 150 [white] soldiers
were also lost. The vast majority of these deaths occurred
prior to the attack as a result of disease. Such losses
significantly hampered the effectiveness of Dunmore's force
and explained his feeble response to the attack.

The events at Gwynn's Island exasperated Lord Dunmore.
His men were weak from illness and demoralized by defeat
and there was little hope of assistance from Britain.
Preparations were made to leave Virginia and join General
Howe's large army in New York. Ships were sent up the
Potomac River to obtain fresh water. They sailed as far as
Stafford County, where they engaged a party of local militia
on the plantation of William Brent. Accounts of the skirmish
vary, but the result was indisputable, the destruction of Brent's
home and the embarrassment of the local militia. The Virginia
Gazette attributed the poor showing of the militia to a lack of
arms:

The disaster which happened at Mr. William Brent's,
on Potowmack river, by the attack made by the
British forces on Tuesday the 23rd of July 1776, was
owing to the militia's not being better armed and
disciplined, and that Capt. James [of the local
militia] kept his ground until his men had all fled

---

[31] Ibid. 10 July, 1777
[32] Ibid.

except about 15; that he attempted several times to rally his men; that the enemy approached under a constant fire of cannon and swivels from a gondola, two sloops and nine boats loaded with men within about 50 yards, before Capt. James left his station....[33]

This small victory was not enough to change Dunmore's decision to leave. In mid-August he abandoned Virginia. Half of his force sailed to St. Augustine, Florida and the other half sailed to New York with Dunmore.[34]

---

[33] Purdie, *Virginia Gazette*, 27 September, 1776
[34] John Selby, *The Revolution in Virginia: 1775-1783*, (Williamsburg, VA: The Colonial Williamsburg Foundation, 1988), 126

Chapter Five

"Great Things [Are] Expected From the Virginians" 1776-1780

Dunmore's departure allowed Virginia to finally send troops north to reinforce General Washington's army in New York. Prior to 1776, only two companies of Virginia riflemen had joined Washington. In mid-August, the 3rd Virginia Regiment marched north to change this. They arrived in New York on September 13th.[1] Captain John Chilton of Fauquier County noted that,

> *Our Regiment reached this place in good spirits and generally speaking healthy, tho not quite full, however; great joy was expressed at our arrival and great things [are] expected from the Virginians, and of consequence we must go through great fatigue and danger.[2]*

Within days of their arrival, the 3rd Virginia participated in a heated skirmish at Harlem Heights. Major Andrew Leitch, of Prince William County, led the regiment's riflemen in a flanking movement against the British. The 3rd Virginia's regimental surgeon proudly described what happened:

---

[1] T. Tripplett Russell and John K. Gott, *Fauquier County in the Revolution*, (Westminster, MD : Willow Bend Books, 1988), 112

[2] Lyon Tyler, "John Chilton to Joseph Blackwell, 13 September, 1776," *Tyler,s Quarterly Historical and Genealogical Magazine, Vol. 12,* (Richmond, VA: Richmond Press Inc., 1931), 91

A very smart action ensued in the true Bush-fighting way...our Troops behaved in a manner that does them the highest Honor. After keeping a very heavy fire on both sides for near three hours they drove the enemy to their main Body and then were prudently ordered to retreat for fear of being drawn into an ambuscade. The 3ʳᵈ Virga. Regt. was ordered out at the Beginning to maintain a particular post in front, and Major Leitch was detached with the 3 Rifle Companies to flank the Enemy. He conducted himself on this occasion in a manner that does him the greatest honor and so did his Party, till he received two balls in his Belly and one In his hip [which proved mortal]...*We had 3 men killed and ten wounded. The Loudon* [County] *Company suffered most – the Captain behaved nobly. Our whole loss is not yet ascertained. The wounded are not more than 40. Coll. Noleton* [Knowlton] *of the N.E. Rangers is the only officer killed. ...Our Battalion (after the Riflemen were detached) were attacked in open field which they drove off and forced them down a Hill...I must mention that the two Yankee Regts. who ran on Sunday fought tollerably well on Monday and in some measure retrieved their reputation. This affair, tho' not great in itself, is of consequence as it gives spirits to the army, which they wanted. Indeed the confusion was such on Sunday that everybody looked dispirited. At present everything wears a different face.*[3]

---

[3] Henry Johnson, "David Griffith to Major Leven Powell, 18 September, 1776," *The Battle of Harlem Heights,*(London: Macmillian, 1897), 171-172

The Mr. Griffith cited by Johnston is incorrectly identified as being a Colonel from Maryland when in fact David Griffith of the 3ʳᵈ Virginia carried on a frequent correspondence with Major Leven Powell during the war.

The improved American morale was only temporary, however. Over the next two months, the British pushed the Americans out of New York and New Jersey. By early December, General Washington's shrinking army had retreated across the Delaware River to Pennsylvania where it briefly found refuge from the British. Washington's men camped along the western bank of the river and reflected on their perilous situation. David Griffith lamented to his friend, Major Levin Powell that,

> We have much need for a speedy re-inforcement. I am much afraid we shall not have it in time to prevent the destruction of American affairs... Everything here wears the face of despondency...A strange consternation seems to have seized everybody in this country. A universal dissatisfaction prevails, and everybody is furnished with an excuse for declining the publick service.[4]

The dissatisfaction that Griffith noticed in Pennsylvania also existed in Virginia. The state struggled to raise men for seven new continental regiments. Fairfax, Prince William, and Loudoun Counties contributed soldiers to three of these regiments. Captain Thomas West, of Fairfax County, commanded a company in Colonel Edward Steven's 10th Virginia Regiment. Loudoun County raised two companies for Colonel Daniel Morgan's 11th Virginia Regiment. They were commanded by Captains William Johnson and William Smith. Prince William County also contributed a company to the 11th Virginia under Captain Charles Galahue. Colonel William Grayson, of Prince William, was given command of a regiment that included soldiers from northern Virginia. Lastly, twenty year old Henry Lee III, of Prince William County, commanded a troop of light dragoons in Colonel

---

[4] Tyler, "David Griffith to Major Powell, 8 December, 1776," 101

Theodorick Bland's cavalry regiment.[5] Unfortunately, none of the units were ready to join Washington in 1776.

The American army huddled along the Delaware River for most of December. General Howe contemplated further pursuit once the river froze, but opted instead to suspend operations and resume the offensive in the spring. In order to obtain comfortable winter quarters for his men, Howe scattered his troops throughout New Jersey. This presented General Washington with one last opportunity to strike the British and boost American morale before his army dissolved.

Trenton

The American strike came on December 26th. Hoping to catch the 1,400 man Hessian garrison in Trenton, New Jersey, by surprise, General Washington devised a daring, multi-pronged attack. The remnants of the continental army, just 2,400 men, many of them Virginians, would cross the Delaware River nine miles above Trenton. At approximately the same time detachments of Pennsylvania militia would cross the river below Trenton. The Americans would converge on Trenton simultaneously and, hopefully, overwhelm the Hessians. The key to the operation was surprise. Washington believed that an attack on the day after Christmas would catch the Hessians off guard. It was also important to coordinate the attack so that all the American units hit Trenton at sunrise. This meant that the river crossings had to occur at night.

On Christmas Day, orders were given to cook three days provisions, draw new flints and ammunition, and prepare to march.[6] The river crossings commenced at sunset. An officer on Washington's staff, probably Colonel John Fitzgerald of

---

[5] Sanchez-Saavedra, 62, 65, 73-74, 102

[6] William Stryker, "General Mercer to Col. Durkee, 25 December, 1776," *The Battles of Trenton and Princeton*, (Republished by The Old Barracks Assoc., Trenton NJ : 2001, Originally published in 1898), 362

Fairfax County, gave a detailed description of the crossing in his diary:

> *Christmas, 6 p.m. -- ...It is fearfully cold and raw and a snow-storm setting in. The wind is northeast and beats in the faces of the men. It will be a terrible night for the soldiers who have no shoes. Some of them have tied old rags around their feet; others are barefoot, but I have not heard a man complain. They are ready to suffer any hardship and die rather than give up their liberty.[7]*

Nine hours later, from across the river, the same officer wrote,

> *Dec. 26, 3 a.m. -- I am writing in the ferry house. The troops are all over, and the boats have gone back for the artillery. We are now three hours behind the set time. Glover's men* (from Massachusetts) *have had a hard time to force the boats through the floating ice with the snow drifting in their faces. I never have seen Washington so determined as he is now. He stands on the bank of the river, wrapped in his cloak, superintending the landing of the troops. He is calm and collected, but very determined. The storm is changing to sleet, and cuts like a knife. The last cannon is being landed, and we are ready to mount our horses.[8]*

Washington's force started its march on Trenton around 4:00 a.m., four hours behind schedule.[9] Although Washington did not know it at the time, the militia units below Trenton had an even harder time crossing the river. They finally gave up, assuming that General Washington had failed as well.

---

[7] Stryker , "Diary of an American Officer on Washington's Staff", 360
[8] Ibid.
[9] Ibid., 139

Far from failing, General Washington was more determined than ever to carry out the attack, and the password for the day, "Victory or Death", emphasized this. An icy winter storm, however, made the march difficult on the men. They pressed forward nonetheless. One observer, Major James Wilkinson, recorded in his memoirs that,

> [The army's] *route was easily traced, as there was a little snow on the ground, which was tinged here and there with blood from the feet of the men who wore broken shoes.*"[10]

About mid-way to Trenton the column split, with General John Sullivan leading half the men down the River Road and General Nathanael Greene taking the other half along the Pennington Road. The plan called for both columns to enter Trenton simultaneously from two directions. As dawn broke, however, Washington's troops were still miles from town, and the element of surprise was in jeopardy.

Fortunately, the same storm that delayed Washington's march caused the Hessians to let down their guard. The first contact between the two sides occurred just outside Trenton, around 8:00 a.m. Major Wilkinson recorded what happened in his diary:

> *It was just 8 o' clock. Looking down the road I saw a Hessian running out from the house. He yelled in Dutch and swung his arms. Three or four others came out with their guns. Two of them fired at us, but the bullets whistled over our heads. Some of General Stephens men rushed forward and captured two.*[11]

---

[10] Ibid. 129
[11] Ibid. 363

The Americans quickly pushed the Hessian pickets into Trenton and seized the high ground overlooking the town. The startled Hessians attempted to form in the streets but were harassed by Washington's artillery. Members of the 3rd Virginia, led by Captain William Washington and Lieutenant James Monroe, swarmed through the streets and overran the Hessians.[12] They were soon pushed to an apple orchard outside of town where they desperately tried to form their lines. The intense American fire took such a toll on their officers, and caused so much confusion in the ranks, that it was impossible to do so.[13] Trapped by the Assunpink Creek in their rear, and the Americans on their front and flanks, the Hessians had little choice but to surrender. They suffered over one hundred casualties, including their commander, Colonel Rall, who died of his wounds the next day.[14] Washington lost just a handful of men.[15] The attack was a staggering success for the Americans, garnering over 900 Hessian prisoners along with much needed supplies.[16] More importantly, the victory provided a huge boost to American morale.

In order to preserve the victory, General Washington's weary army marched back to McKonkey's Ferry, re-crossed the river, and collapsed on the other side. It had been an exhausting, yet decisive two days.

News of Washington's victory quickly spread throughout the region and revived the flagging morale of Americans. While the army rested, General Washington learned that General Howe had withdrawn his troops to central New Jersey. Washington decided to fill the vacuum left by their departure. On December 30th, the American army re-crossed the river and encamped in Trenton. News of the crossing prompted General Howe to move with uncharacteristic speed.

---

[12] Ibid. 164
[13] Ibid. 186
[14] Ibid. 195
[15] Ibid. 196
[16] Ibid. 386

He sent approximately 8,000 men under General Cornwallis to destroy Washington's army.[17] The stage was sent for round two.

Princeton

General Washington expected the British to attack him at Trenton and positioned his men along the bank of the Assunpink Creek, south of town. He concentrated his artillery on a bridge that spanned the creek. On January 2nd, reinforcements arrived under General John Cadwalader swelling Washington's army to approximately 6,000 men.[18]

Reports that a strong British force was in Princeton prompted General Washington to place a strong detachment along the Princeton Road to harass and retard their advance to Trenton. The detachment included the remnants of three Virginia regiments (the 4th, 5th and 6th Virginia Regiments), a regiment of Continental riflemen, and six field pieces.[19]

Part of this blocking force was posted along Shabbakonk Creek, about three miles from Trenton. They were hidden in thick woods along the creek and staggered Cornwallis's vanguard with a fierce volley when they approached. General Cornwallis spent precious time, and daylight, deploying his main body of troops and slowly drove the Americans out of the woods and towards Trenton. When they reached the outskirts of town, the American advance guard made another stand. General Washington arrived on the scene and urged the

[17] Samuel S. Smith, *The Battle of Princeton*, (Monmouth Beach, NJ : Philip Freneau Press, 1967), 12

[18] Smith, *The Battle of Princeton*, 13

[19] Dennis P Ryan, "Robert Beale Memoirs," *A Salute to Courage: The American Revolution as Seen Through Wartime Writings of Officers of the Continental Army and Navy*, (NY: Columbia University Press, 1979), 56 and James Wilkinson, *Memoirs of My Own Times, Vol.* 1 (Philadelphia: Abraham Small, 1816), 135

advance troops to hold the line as long as possible. Major Wilkinson recalled that,

> *General Washington...feeling how important it was to retard the march of the enemy until nightfall...thanked the detachment, and particularly the artillery, for the services of the day, gave orders for as obstinate a stand as could be made on that ground, without hazarding the [artillery] pieces, and retired to marshal his troops for action, behind the Assanpink.*"[20]

A thirty-minute artillery duel ensued, but the British eventually overwhelmed the Americans and continued their advance. Ensign Robert Beale of Virginia recalled,

> [Major Forsyth] *ordered to the right about face on and off in order. We had not taken more than regular steps until the word, 'Shift for yourselves, boys, get over the bridge as quick as you can.' There was running followed by a tremendous fire from the British.*[21]

The Americans raced through town, crossed the Assunpink Bridge, and waited with the rest of Washington's troops for Cornwallis to strike.

The gravity of the moment weighed heavily on everyone. Ensign Beale recalled,

> *This was a most awful crisis. No possible chance of crossing the river; ice as large as houses floating down, and no retreat to the mountains, the British between us and them. Our brigade, consisting of the Fourth, Fifth, and Sixth Virginia Regiments, was ordered to form in column at the bridge and General*

---

[20] Ibid. 138
[21] Ryan (Robert Beale Memoirs), 56

> *Washington came and, in the presence of us all, told Colonel Scott to defend the bridge to the last extremity. Colonel Scott answered with an oath, 'Yes, General, as long as there is a man alive.'*[22]

Major Wilkinson also noted the urgency of the situation:

> *If ever there was a crisis in the affairs of the revolution this was the moment ; thirty minutes would have sufficed to bring the two armies into contact, and thirty more would have decided the combat....*[23]

British and Hessian troops mounted three charges against the bridge, but each charge was repulsed by a barrage of American artillery and small arms fire. The Americans would not budge, and with the last rays of daylight fading in the west, General Cornwallis decided to suspend his attack and resume it in the morning. The Virginians, along with Washington's artillery, had bought the army a twelve hour reprieve, and Washington made full use of it.

Around midnight, after a few hours of tense rest, most of the American army quietly withdrew from the lines and marched along a little used back road towards Princeton. Washington hoped to surprise the small British garrison there with a dawn attack. The maneuver required stealth and deception. About 400 local militia remained in the American lines at Trenton to maintain the appearance of an army preparing for battle.[24] They kept the campfires burning and continued to dig earthworks to convince the British that Washington was still there. The ruse worked; only a handful of British sentries reported movement in the American camp, but these reports went unheeded by British officers .

---

[22] Ryan, (Robert Beale Memoirs), 56
[23] Wilkinson, 138
[24] Stryker, 275

The night march to Princeton, like the one to Trenton a week earlier, was difficult on the men. One soldier recalled,

> *Our men were without shoes or other comfortable clothing; and as traces of our march towards Princeton, the ground was literally marked with the blood of the soldiers feet.*[25]

As the Americans approached the outskirts of Princeton around sunrise, General Washington split his force. General Greene was sent to the left to secure a bridge at Stony Brook and enter Princeton along the Post Road, while General Sullivan continued along the back road with the bulk of the army. General Greene's column consisted of a brigade under General Hugh Mercer (between 300-350 men) and a much larger brigade under General Cadwalader (approximately 1,150). [26] Mercer's brigade included riflemen from Colonel Rawlings's Virginia/Maryland Rifle Regiment, Colonel Miles's Pennsylvania Rifle Regiment, a handful of Virginia and Delaware continentals, and the remnants of the 1st Maryland Regiment.[27]

At almost the same moment that Washington divided his army, a British column about a mile to the west crossed the Stony Brook Bridge and ascended a hill on their way to Trenton. They were reinforcements (over 400) from the 17th and 55th British Regiments under Lieutenant Colonel Charles Mawhood.[28] As they climbed the hill, some of Mawhood's

---

[25] Sergeant R, "The Battle of Princeton," *The Pennsylvania Magazine of History and Biography, Vol. 20, No. 1* (1896), 515

[26] Wilkinson, 141, See also:
Caesar Rodney, *The Diary of Captain Thomas Rodney, 1776-1777,* (Wilmington: The Historical Society of Delaware, 1888), 33
David Hackett Fischer, *Washington's Crossing* (Oxford Univiversity Press, 2004), 408 and
Samuel Smith, *Princeton,* 34

[27] Fischer, 408

[28] Smith, *Princeton,* 19

horsemen caught a glimpse of Sullivan's column moving towards Princeton. Mawhood could not determine the size of the American force, but realized that the lone British regiment still in Princeton, the 40th, was in danger, so he reversed direction and rapidly marched back to town. General Washington, who was with Sullivan, soon learned about Mawhood's column. He assumed that it was only a British reconnaissance force from Princeton and ordered General Mercer to pursue and attack it before it warned the town's garrison.[29] Mercer responded quickly; he marched his brigade up a hill to the right and attempted to head off the British.[30]

General Mercer's men collided with a party of Mawhood's dismounted dragoons in an orchard outside of town. A soldier in Mercer's detachment, known to history only as Sergeant R, described what happened:

> *As we were descending a hill through an orchard, a party of the enemy who were entrenched behind a bank and fence, rose and fired upon us. Their first shot passed over our heads cutting the limbs of the trees under which we were marching. At this moment we were ordered to wheel...We formed, advanced and fired upon the enemy. They retreated eight rods to their packs, which were laid in a line. I advanced to the fence of the opposite side of the ditch which the enemy had just left, fell on one knee and loaded my musket with ball and buckshot. Our fire was destructive; their ranks grew thin and the victory seemed nearly complete, when the British were reinforced.*[31]

Note: Fischer contends that the Mawhood's column was closer to 700 men, 329

[29] Smith, *Princeton,* 20
[30] Ibid.
[31] Sergeant R, 517

Mercer's men pushed Mawhood's dragoons back, but now they faced Mawhood's whole force, over 300 strong. Lieutenant James McMichael of the Pennsylvania rifle battalion recalled the encounter:

> *Gen. Mercer, with 100 Pennsylvania riflemen and 20 Virginians, was detached to the front to bring on the attack. The enemy then consisting of 500 [actually closer to 300] paraded in an open field in battle array. We boldly marched to within 25 yards of them, and then commenced the attack, which was very hot. We kept up an incessant fire until it came to pushing bayonets, when we were ordered to retreat.[32]*

Many of Mercer's men lacked bayonets and fled to the rear when the British advanced. They abandoned two cannon and their commander, who was struck down and mortally wounded by British bayonets.

Help soon arrived for Mercer's scattered troops in the form of General Cadwalader's Pennsylvania militiamen and an artillery battery under Captain William Moulder. They momentarily checked the British advance, but withdrew when Mawhood resumed his attack. All that remained of the American line was Moulder's artillery, protected by a few intrepid infantrymen under Captain Thomas Rodney of Delaware.

Their determined stand stalled the British advance and allowed Cadwalder's and Mercer's brigades to reform. Reinforcements from General Sullivan's column, accompanied by General Washington, also arrived and helped turn the battle. At great danger to himself, Washington rallied Cadwalader's and Mercer's men. Sergeant R observed that,

---

[32] James McMichael, "The Diary of Lt. James McMichael of the Pennsylvania Line, 1776-1778," *The Pennsylvania Magazine of History and Biography, Vol. 16, No. 2*, 1892,   141

Washington appeared in front of the American army, riding towards those of us who were retreating, and exclaimed 'Parade with us, my brave fellows, there is but a handful of the enemy, and we will have them directly.[33]

The effect of his appeal was electric. Sergeant R recalled, "*I immediately joined the main body, and marched over the ground again.*"[34] Washington led the restored American line forward. Mawhood's troops momentarily resisted, but were significantly outflanked and began to retreat. When a large party of American riflemen moved against their left flank, the British retreat turned into a rout. Major Wilkinson noted that, "*the riflemen were...the first in pursuit, and in fact took the greatest part of the prisoners.*"[35] They were urged on by General Washington who gleefully exclaimed, "*It's a fine fox chase, boys!*"[36]

Many of Colonel Mawhood's men sought shelter in Nassau Hall, a large brick building in town. A blast of artillery quickly convinced them to surrender, however, and Washington's victory was complete. At the cost of less than forty men killed, including General Mercer who died of his wounds a few days later, and another forty wounded, the Americans inflicted a second stunning defeat on General Howe's army. British losses in killed, wounded, and captured numbered between 400 to 500 men.[37]

General Washington was tempted to stage one more daring assault on an important British supply depot at New Brunswick. He decided against it, however, because his men were exhausted and in no condition to face Cornwallis, who

---

[33] Sergeant R, 517
[34] Ibid.
[35] Wilkinson, 145
[36] Ibid.
[37] Fischer, 414-415
   Note: General Mercer died of his wounds a few days after the battle.

was rapidly marching eastward from Trenton. Reluctantly, Washington headed north, towards Morristown, and the safety of New Jersey's mountains.

The Home Front

While Washington's army struggled on the battlefields of New Jersey, the situation in Virginia was relatively stable. Lord Dunmore's departure in August ushered in a period of calm. As fear of British raids subsided, most of the militia stationed along the Potomac returned to their homes.

Word of Washington's victories at Trenton and Princeton reached Virginia in January and electrified the state. British visitor Nicholas Cresswell noted the impact of the news:

Loudoun County, January 16-17, 1777

News that Washington had taken 760 Hessian prisoners at Trenton...is confirmed...The minds of the people are much altered. A few days ago they had given up the cause for lost. Their late success have turned the scale and now they are all liberty mad again. Their Recruiting parties could not get a man...and now the men are coming in by companies. Confound the [Hessians]...This has given them new spirits, got them fresh succours, and will prolong the war, perhaps for two years.[38]

While fresh recruits joined new regiments, Prince William County prepared to welcome some unwilling guests. In mid January, Congress decreed that the Hessians captured at Trenton would be held in Dumfries.[39] The captives arrived in January and were granted a considerable degree of autonomy. One Hessian officer noted that,

---

[38] Cresswell Journal, 179-180
[39] Journals of Congress, January 14, 1777

Dumfries is a little place of fifty to sixty houses and an unhealthy place because of a marsh nearby. However, it has a strong tobacco business and there are rather large boats or sloops in [Quantico] Creek...In the beginning we lodged in an inn, but the innkeeper scrimped so much that it was impossible to subsist. So I found quarters about a mile from the town with a man named Bennett, and began my own economy, whereby I fared much better. For quarters and bed I paid seven shillings a week, Virginia money....[40]

When the officer's money ran out, however, his captivity became uncomfortable:

At Dumfries I moved into the town again...But I had neither bed, nor chair, nor table, still less a pot for cooking, still less a vessel with which I could fetch water, eat out of and drink. Therefore, I had to live for a while like Robinson Crusoe on his island until I could rummage up something for hard money. For a whole month my bed was an armful of hay on which lay a musquetir tent...and over me a thin woolen blanket.[41]

The officer's condition improved with the help of one of the town's residents:

Finally my former innkeeper loaned me a little pot for cooking and I bought an earthen plate jug from a shopkeeper for 2 shillings, as well as an earthen

---

[40] C.W. Heckert, "Wiederholt Diary, 24 January, 1777," *A German-American Diary: Notes of Related Historical Interest, Including Translated Excerpts from the Wiederholdt Diary,* (Parsons, WV : McClain Printing Co., 1980), 148

[41] Ibid., "20 February, 777", 150

plate and cup, together with a little casserole of the same material. Thus I carried on my housekeeping, cooked, ate and drank what I had and wanted to. I lived pleasurably in that way, better than those who lived and ate in public taverns and with private individuals, for which they paid [enormously] and went into debt...I could save some money; I lived in my customary German style, ate at the regular time, went to bed at the right time, and got up at the regular time.[42]

In July, concern about a possible British rescue of the Hessians prompted Congress to move most of the prisoners to the interior of the state. Colonel Henry Lee II, the commander of Prince William County's militia, was ordered *"to remove all the Hessian Privates to Winchester, under a proper escort, leaving with the field officers all their necessary attendants."*[43] The Hessian officers joined their men in Winchester in September.

Dumfries was more than just a prison camp in 1777. In the spring, the town, along with Alexandria, was a center for smallpox inoculations. The disease ravaged both armies in 1776, and General Washington hoped inoculations would prevent a re-occurence in 1777. Inoculations were conducted at the American encampment in Morristown, New Jersey as well as in Philadelphia, Baltimore, Alexandria, and Dumfries. On April 6th, George Mason noted that,

The whole towns of Dumfries and Alexandria are under inoculation for the small pox, in the latter about 600 persons....[44]

---

[42] Ibid.

[43] H. R. McILwaine, ed., *Journals of the Council of the State of Virginia, Vol. 1*, (Richmond, 1931), 452

[44] Rutland, "George Mason to Patrick Henry," *The Papers of George Mason, Vol. 1*, 336

The inoculations took nearly a month to recover from and were administered all spring. George Mason joined the ranks of the inoculated in May and, like most recipients, emerged unscathed.[45]

Smallpox was not the only concern of Virginians. Many were *"greatly alarmed at the HIGH PRICE of every commodity"*.[46] Widespread shortages drove prices upwards, and inflation affected everyone, including the Hessian prisoners. One officer observed that, *"all is now dear and there is nothing to be had."*[47] There was little that could be done, however, as the war disrupted trade and commerce in all the states.

Militia Service in 1777

One cause of the economic and social disruption in Virginia was frequent sightings of British ships off the coast. Such sightings usually prompted alarms and militia mobilizations. Fairfax, Loudoun, and Prince William Counties called out their militia numerous times in 1777 to defend against marauding British ships in the Potomac River. Virginians were particularly concerned about the safety of Mrs. Washington. Militia troops from Fairfax and Prince William Counties were frequently posted at Mount Vernon to protect the General's family and home.[48] One militiaman from Fairfax County recalled many visits to Mount Vernon:

---

[45] Rutland, "George Mason to George Wythe, 14 June, 1777," *The Papers of George Mason, Vol. 1,* 345 and Journals of the Continental Congress, April 22 and 30, 1777

[46] Rutland, "From the Voters of Fairfax County," *The Papers of George Mason, Vol. 1,* 346-47

[47] Wiederholdt Diary, "15 April, 1777," 152

[48] Dorman, "John Burch Pension Application," *Virginia Revolutionary Pension Applications, Vol. 12,* 88
  See also: "Joshua Ferguson Pension Application," *Vol. 36,* 57 and
  "Richard Gray Pension Application," *Vol. 46,* 68

Upon several occasions they marched to Gen. Washington's house to protect it, where they would remain for several weeks at a time, and sometimes to Alexandria where the company spent several months at one time in building batteries for cannon for the defense of the town.[49]

Troops also assembled in Dumfries and other vulnerable locations along the river. A militia soldier from Loudoun County recalled that,

In Sept. 1777 Capt. Lewis' company was called into service for the purpose of protecting the country along the shores of the Potomac. He rendezvoused at Leesburg and served three months. He marched to Alexandria where they stayed a short time and then marched down the Potomac River to deter the British from landing and plundering the country.[50]

Another militiaman from Prince William County noted that,

He entered the service in April 1777...He was drafted for sixty days and ordered to rendezvous at Dumfries...He marched down the river in pursuit of the British as low as Gen. Washington's fishing bay where they were stationed about fifteen days. They then marched to the high point on the Potomac River where they stayed a few days and then to Occoquan Creek where they remained until [his sixty day commitment] expired.[51]

---

[49] Dorman, "Joshua Ferguson Pension Application," *Virginia Revolutionary Pension Applications Vol. 36,* 57

[50] Dorman, "Samuel Conn Pension Application," *Virginia Revolutionary Pension Applications Vol. 21,* 84

[51] Dorman, "William Brewer Pension Application, *Virginia Revolutionary Pension Applications, Vol. 10,* 18

Although British raiding parties frequently alarmed northern Virginians, the state was spared the destruction of war in 1777. British operations centered around Philadelphia and upstate New York. In late August, General Howe landed approximately 15,000 troops at Head of Elk, Maryland, and marched towards Philadelphia. General Washington, who rebuilt the continental army in 1777, matched Howe's strength and positioned his army to intercept the British at Brandywine Creek. The scene was set for one of the war's biggest clashes, and hundreds of northern Virginia continentals played a crucial role in the battle.

Battle of Brandywine

The battle of Brandywine began early in the morning of September 11th, 1777. The British plan of attack was for General Knyphausen, with nearly 7,000 men, to feint an attack along the American front at Chadd's Ford, while General Howe led a force of over 8,000 men on a march around the American right flank.[52]

General William Maxwell, of New Jersey, commanded an 800 man American light corps a few miles west of Chadd's Ford. At 7:00 a.m. Maxwell's advance guard, commanded by Captain Charles Porterfield of the 11th Virginia Regiment, hit Knyphausen's vanguard with a well-aimed volley. Porterfield's instructions were to, *"deliver his fire as soon as he should meet the van of the enemy and then fall back"*.[53] His company did precisely that, dropping a number of enemy soldiers.

Porterfield's men retreated and reformed on the next American position, once again pouring a close and destructive fire on the British.[54] This fighting withdrawal went on all

---

[52] Samuel Smith, *The Battle of Brandywine*, (Philip Freneau Press : Monmouth Beach, NJ, 1976), 9
[53] Ibid. 10
[54] Ibid.

morning with Maxwell's men using trees and stone walls for cover and grudgingly yielding ground. Eventually, the strength of the British attack was too great for the Americans and they withdrew to the main American line at Chadd's Ford.[55]

The 3rd Virginia, attached to General William Woodford's brigade of General Adam Stephen's Division, was stationed a few miles upstream from Chadd's Ford. They heard the morning fight draw closer and braced for the full force of a British attack, but it never materialized. The enemy seemed content to hold their position across the creek.

Confusion reigned at Washington's headquarters as he received conflicting reports of enemy troop movements. Around 2:00 p.m., Washington realized that the British had marched around his right flank and threatened his whole army. He ordered Generals Stirling, Stephen, and Sullivan to reposition their troops in order to face the enemy. Washington's entire right flank thus bent at a right angle to its original position. The Americans scrambled to the heights near Birmingham Meeting House, just ahead of the British and prepared to meet their attack.

General William Woodford's brigade of Virginians deployed on a hill about two hundred yards southwest of the Birmingham Meetinghouse. They held the extreme right of the American line. This meant that the brigade's own right flank was uncovered. General Woodford sent the 170 men of the 3rd Virginia to an orchard north of the Meetinghouse to screen his vulnerable flank. The men crossed a deep vale and took position amongst the fruit trees. A mile to their front sat thousands of enemy troops, resting from their seventeen mile march. The 3rd Virginians were ordered, *"to hold the wood*

---

[55] John F. Reed, *Campaign to Valley Forge, July 1, 1777 – December 19, 1777*, (Philadelphia: University of Pennsylvania Press, 1965), 120

as long as it was tenable & then retreat to the right of the brigade."[56]

Fighting erupted at Birmingham around 3:30 p.m. when the British advance guard approached the orchard. According to a British officer, the advance guard, *"received the fire from about 200 men in an orchard."*[57] This unexpected American resistance caused the British to take cover behind a fence, two hundred paces from the orchard.[58] Captain Johann Ewald, of the German Jagers, noted that,

> *About half past three I caught sight of some infantry and horsemen behind a village on a hill in the distance. I drew up at once and deployed...I reached the first houses of the village with the flankers of the jagers, and Lt. Hagen followed me with the horsemen. But unfortunately for us, the time this took favored the enemy and I received extremely heavy small-arms fire from the gardens and houses, through which, however, only two jagers were wounded. Everyone ran back, and I formed them again behind the fences or walls at a distance of two hundred paces from the village....*[59]

General George Weedon applauded the conduct of his former regiment and claimed that its commander, Colonel Thomas Marshall,

---

[56] Brigadier General George Weedon's Correspondence Account of the Battle of Brandywine, 11 September, 1777. The original manuscript letter is in the collections of the Chicago Historical Society. Transcribed by Bob McDonald, 2001.

[57] Smith, 16

[58] Ibid. 17

[59] Captain Johann Ewald, *Diary of the American War: A Hessian Journal*, (New Haven & London: Yale Univ. Press, 1979), 84-85 Translated & edited by Joseph P. Tustin.

Received the Enemy with a Firmness which will do Honor to him & his little Corps, as long as the 11th of Sepr. is remembered. He continued there ¾ of one Hour, & must have done amazing execution.[60]

General Light Horse Harry Lee, writing about the battle years latter, concurred, noting that the 3rd Virginia,

Bravely sustained itself against superior numbers, never yielding one inch of ground and expending thirty rounds a man, in forty-five minutes.[61]

Even the main British battleline, upon arriving at the advance guard's position, was forced to halt momentarily to seek cover. One British officer reported that the American fire was so intense that,

The trees (were) cracking over ones head. The branches riven by the artillery, the leaves falling as in autumn by the grapeshot.[62]

The British eventually overwhelmed the Virginians and pushed them out of the orchard. Colonel Marshall repositioned his men approximately one hundred paces to the rear, behind a stone wall at the Birmingham Meetinghouse. The 3rd Virginia maintained such a heavy fire from behind the wall that the attacking British forces were compelled to veer around their flanks.[63]

Fearing that the 3rd Virginia was about to be surrounded, General Woodford ordered its withdrawal. The regiment joined the American army in a general retreat.[64] The fight

---

[60] Weedon Correspondence, 11 September, 1777
[61] Henry Lee, *The Revolutionary War Memoirs of General Henry Lee,* (New York: Da Capo Press, Originally Published in 1812), 89-90
[62] Smith, 17
[63] Ibid. 18
[64] Weedon Correspondence, 11 September, 1777

resumed on a second hill, a half mile in the rear, but again the Americans were forced back. Fortunately, General Nathanael Greene's division, comprised largely of Virginians under Generals George Weedon and Peter Muhlenberg, arrived in time to provide cover for the retreating Americans. The British ended their pursuit at sunset, in possession of the field, and victory. American losses in killed, wounded, and captured, were approximately 1,300, more than double the roughly 600 casualties of the British.[65] Perhaps even more disturbing was that three weeks later, Philadelphia fell to the British without a fight.

Militia Reinforcements for Washington: 1777

A few days before the battle of Brandywine, General Washington had urged the states to send him reinforcements. Virginia responded to Washington's appeal with a militia draft. Governor Patrick Henry ordered the northern counties, including Fairfax, Loudoun, and Prince William, to

> *Draw out one third part of the militia...to be on Continental pay...and to march them to Frederick Town in Maryland; there to wait the orders of General Washington.*[66]

All three counties complied and sent troops north in September. They arrived too late to fight at Brandywine and just missed Washington's unsuccessful attack at Germantown in early October. Nonetheless, the 1,100 men were much needed reinforcements.[67] The troops from Fairfax were commanded by Colonel William Rumney and attached to

---

[65] Reed, 140

[66] McIlwaine, *Journals of the Council of the State of Virginia, Vol. 1*, 478

[67] Philander D. Chase and Edward G. Lengel, "General Washington to John Hancock, 10 October, 1777," *The Papers of George Washington, Vol. 11*, 474

General Charles Scott's brigade. The Prince William and Loudoun County militia troops joined others from Culpeper and Berkely Counties to form a brigade under Colonel William Crawford.[68] Unfortunately, many of the Virginians were poorly armed and supplied. Even worse, their militia service was short, just three months. Most returned to Virginia before Washington entered Valley Forge in December.

Plenty of northern Virginians remained with Washington as winter approached. They were members of Virginia's continental regiments and were encamped at Whitemarsh, thirteen miles north of Philadelphia. General Washington realized that his army was too weak to dislodge the British from the capital, yet, he was determined to remain close and harass the enemy when they ventured out of their fortified lines. General Howe, on the other hand, was content to let the Americans linger. He had accomplished his objective, the capture of Philadelphia. If General Washington wished to remain in the field and expose his men to the hardships of winter, so be it. The British would spend a cozy winter in Philadelphia, and finish off the American army in the spring.

Weather conditions gradually deteriorated and caused much suffering in the American ranks. Lieutenant John Marshall noted that,

> *The cold was now becoming so intense that it was impossible for an army, neither well clothed, nor sufficiently supplied with blankets, to keep the field in tents.*[69]

Washington thus decided to end the campaign and establish winter quarters at Valley Forge.

---

[68] See: Chase and Lengel, "Gen. Orders for 6 October and 11 October, 1777," *The Papers of George Washington, Vol.* 11, 404, 481
[69] Marshall, 354

Valley Forge

The army marched into Valley Forge with few provisions. General James Varnum, of Rhode Island, reported to General Washington on December 22nd that,

> *Three Days successively, we have been destitute of Bread. Two Days we have been intirely without Meat. – It is not to be had from Commissaries. – Whenever we procure Beef, it is of such a vile Quality, as to render it a poor Succedanium for Food. The Men must be supplied, or they cannot be commanded.*[70]

General Washington passed the bad news on to Congress.

> *I do not know from what cause this alarming deficiency, or rather total failure of Supplies arises: But unless more vigorous exertions and better regulations take place in that line and immediately, This Army must dissolve.*[71]

The lack of supplies contributed to a startling drop in the number of men fit for duty. The Virginia continental line, like the entire American army, was a mere shadow of itself. Of the 1,287 men listed on the January roll of General William Woodford's brigade, only 231 were present and fit for duty.[72] The other Virginia brigades had similar numbers. Although some of the missing men were on detached service, a full two thirds of them were sick, on furlough, or unfit for service due

---

[70] Joseph Lee Boyle, *Writings from the Valley Forge Encampment of the Continental Army Vol. 1*, (Bowie MD: Heritage Books Inc., 2000), 2
[71] General Washington to Henry Laurens, 22 December, 1777 in *The Papers of George Washington, Vol. 12*, 667
[72] Charles H. Lesser, ed. *The Sinews of Independence: Monthly Strength Reports of the Continental Army*, (Chicago: The University of Chicago Press, 1976), 58

to inadequate clothing.[73]   As February approached, the Virginia brigades shrank further. The two year enlistments of about half of Virginia's regiments expired in early 1778 and many of the men were eager to return home. By the end of February, General Woodford's entire brigade totaled 119 men fit for duty, and only 57 of them were privates.[74]

These men endured the worst part of Valley Forge. The supply system, which barely functioned in January, completely failed in February.

> *"A moments Opportunity presents of telling you our Distress in Camp has been infinite,"* wrote Alexander Scammell on February 19th. *"In all the Scenes since I have been in the army, want of provisions these ten Days past, has been the most distressing; [a] great part of our Troops 7 Days with only half a pound of Pork during the whole time –Our poor brave Soldiers living upon bread & water & naked exhibited a Sight exceedingly affecting to the Officers."*[75]

William Weeks, the paymaster of the 3rd New Hampshire Regiment, expressed similar concerns.

> *The first thing I must enter upon is the Scarcity of Provision here.   Death seem'd to stare the poor Soldiers in the Face; for this five Days the Soldiers have not drawn [a] Tenth Part of their Allowance.*[76]

Even General Washington noted the hardship, writing to George Clinton, of New York, for assistance.

---

[73] Ibid.
[74] Lesser, 59
[75] Joseph Lee Boyle, *Writings from the Valley Forge Encampment of the Continental Army Vol. 2*, (Bowie MD: Heritage Books Inc., 2001), 50
[76] Boyle, *Writings from the Valley Forge Encampment of the Continental Army Vol. 1*, 55

For some days past, there has been little less, than a famine in camp. A part of the army has been a week, without any kind of flesh, and the rest three or four days. Naked and starving as they are, we cannot enough admire the incomparable patience and fidelity of the soldiery, that they have not been ere this excited by their sufferings, to a general mutiny and dispersion. Strong symptoms, however, of discontent have appeared in particular instances; and nothing but the most active efforts every where can long avert so shocking a catastrophe.[77]

Thankfully, the crisis passed in the spring when more provisions found their way to camp.

With the approach of spring, the camp routine changed. Work on the entrenchments continued, as did fatigue and guard duty. But the arrival of Baron von Steuben, from Europe, meant that the men would soon learn a new military drill.

Steuben arrived in Valley Forge in late February and immediately impressed General Washington with his military knowledge and humility.[78] Washington asked the Baron to assess the American army.[79] Steuben's observations were the beginning of significant reforms for the American army.

"I directed my attention to the condition of the troops," recalled Steuben years later, *"and found ample field, where disorder and confusion were supreme...the words company, regiment, brigade, and division, were so vague that they did not convey any idea upon which to form a calculation...I have*

---

[77] "General Washington to George Clinton, 16 February, 1778," *The Papers of George Washington Vol. 13*, 552-553

[78] John W. Jackson, *Valley Forge, Pinnacle of Courage*, (Gettysburg: PA, Thomas Publications, 1992), 124

[79] Ibid. 126

seen a regiment consisting of thirty men, and a company of one corporal!"[80]

Steuben was particularly critical of the haphazard system of drill the army employed.

Each colonel had a system of his own, the one according to the English, the other according to the Prussian or French style.[81]

His keen observations prompted General Washington to ask him to oversee the implementation of reforms. Steuben immediately went to work. John Marshall summarized Baron von Steuben's impact on the American army.

This gentleman was a real service to the American troops. He established one uniform system of field exercise; and, by his skill and persevering industry, effected important improvements through all ranks of the army during its continuance at Valley Forge.[82]

The advent of April brought a surge of men to the ranks. General Woodford's brigade swelled to 470 men fit for duty. By June, the brigade numbered almost 650 men. Some of these men were northern Virginians, pledged to serve for three years. They were destined to participate in the longest battle of the war, Monmouth, and one of the most daring American attacks of the war, Stony Point. Unfortunately, many of the men were also destined to be part of America's single greatest defeat of the war, the fall of Charleston, South Carolina in 1780.

---

[80] Friedrich Kapp, *The Life of Frederick William von Steuben*, (NY: Corner house Historical Publications, 1999), 115 (Originally published in 1859)
[81] Ibid. 118
[82] John Marshall, *The Life of George Washington, Vol.* 2 (Fredericksburg, VA: The Citizens Guild of Washington's Boyhood Home, 1926), 439

Alarms Along the Potomac : 1777-1780

Although there was little combat in Virginia between 1777-1780, service in the local militia was surprisingly active. British ships continued to visit Chesapeake Bay, sparking numerous alarms. William Brewer's pension account of his service with the Prince William County militia was typical:

In June 1778 the British...ascended the Potomac River...[A] draft was made for twenty days. He marched...under [Colonel] Harry Lee...to Bullit's Bay...After a short time the enemy disappeared and they marched to the mouth of Chapawamsick Creek where a breast work was ordered thrown up by Col. Jesse Ewell. To accomplish this they were laboriously employed till the twenty days were out then he was discharged...

In 1779 the British again made their appearance in the Potomac River. A draft for thirty days took place...In May 1779 he marched...to the mouth of Chapawamsick Creek where he was stationed to prevent the British from landing and provide some security to the inhabitants near the river. In Sept. 1779 another call for thirty days was made. He marched under the same officers to Chapawamsick encampment where he was discharged...

In the spring of 1780 when the British appeared again he was called out for thirty days under his former officers. In May they marched to the Potomac River to prevent the enemy from landing. After traversing the river they again went to Chapawamsick. In Oct. 1780 he was called out for thirty days and marched from Prince William County...to the Potomac River to defend the shores from the enemy as it was their constant practice to land and plunder when they could do it with safety.[83]

Another Prince William County militia veteran, Levi Davis, recalled in his pension application that,

> *He volunteered in 1778 to prevent the British from landing so frequently and at so many places that he cannot describe the details of each campaign.*[84]

The same was true for members of the Fairfax militia. Joshua Ferguson recalled several instances where he marched to Mount Vernon and Alexandria to fend off British ships:

> *This species of service continued pretty much from 1778 until the end of the war, as the British ships visited the Potomac during that time frequently for the purpose of plunder and annoyance....*[85]

Although these raids caused some economic loss and disruption, they proved militarily insignificant. Ferguson noted that,

> *He never was in any action with the enemy who were generally near their ships and would retire upon the appearance of the American forces.*[86]

---

[83] Dorman, "William Brewer Pension Application," *Virginia Revolutionary Pension Applications, Vol. 10,* 18

[84] Dorman, "Levi Davis Pension Application," *Virginia Revolutionary Pension Applications, Vol. 27,* 86

[85] Dorman, "Joshua Ferguson Pension Application," *Virginia Revolutionary Pension Applications, Vol. 36,* 57

[86] Ibid.

Assisting the Carolinas

Militia service for northern Virginians was not limited to the Potomac River. Militia companies were sent south in 1780 to reinforce the small American army in South Carolina under General Nathanael Greene. George Mason's son, William, led a company from Fairfax County. Mason recalled,

> *The Men are mostly Volunteers; who turned out from the Battalion at large...there are among them Several Soldiers, and three or four Serjeants who had served out their Time in the Virginia Line on Continental Establishment; so that I look upon it to be equal to any Militia Company in the state.*[87]

Jesse Dailey, of Fairfax County, served in Captain William Mason's company and noted in his pension application that,

> *They marched from Colchester on 7 October [1780] and passed through Dumfries, Fredericksburg, Richmond and Petersburg and to Hillsborough N.C. where they formed the regiment under Gen. [Edward] Stephens...They marched from Hillsborough through Guilford Court House, Salisbury, Charlotte, and to South Carolina on the Pee Dee River. They crossed the river on Christmas Day...Their fare there was one-half gill of whiskey and parched corn. The next day they marched to Cheraw Hills where they stayed until sometime in January....*[88]

---

[87] Boyd, "George Mason to Thomas Jefferson, 6 October, 1780," *The Papers of Thomas Jefferson, Vol. 4,* 18

[88] Dorman, "Jesse Dailey Pension Application," *Virginia Revolutionary Pension Applications, Vol. 26,* 31-31

Prince William County also sent a company of militia to South Carolina under Captain John Britt. Private Daniel Cole recounted that,

> *The company was detained some three weeks or more on the road awaiting reinforcements from other counties...[At Roanoke] huts were erected and the soldiers were stationed. [Cole] Was there nearly a month. Then his company was ordered south...They were stationed [at Cheraw Hills, SC] about three months. While there [Cole] performed numerous trips into the country in search of the enemy....*[89]

Joseph Bobo, another Prince William County private, recalled:

> *His company was poorly provided with tents and during the winter their shelters were covered with pine branch. The suffering from cold, however, was not very severe.*[90]

Their stay in Cheraw Hills, South Carolina was relatively uneventful. This was especially true in comparison to the American troops under General Daniel Morgan. Morgan commanded a detached corps of light infantry in South Carolina. On January 17th, 1781, Morgan scored a decisive victory over the British at the Battle of Cowpens. To prevent the re-capture of approximately 800 British prisoners by General Cornwallis, Morgan headed north towards Virginia.

Since the term of service for most of the Virginia militia in the Carolinas was nearly expired, they were chosen to escort the captives north. They arrived at Pittsylvania Court House in February where all but the few volunteers -- who agreed to escort the prisoners to Charlottesville -- returned home.

---

[89] Dorman, "Daniel Cole Pension Application," *Virginia Revolutionary Pension Applications, Vol. 20,* 75

[90] Dorman, "Joseph Bobo Pension Application," *Virginia Revolutionary Pension Applications, Vol. 8,* 6

Chapter Six

"A Few Weeks Exertions and the Enemy is Expelled from Our State Forever" 1781

The war returned to Virginia in 1781 with the arrival of a British expedition under the command of the infamous American traitor, Benedict Arnold. On December 31st, 1780, word reached Governor Thomas Jefferson, in Richmond, that a number of ships were off the Virginia Capes. Their identity and destination were unknown, so Jefferson responded cautiously. With most of the state's militia weary of the frequent alarms and service in the Carolinas, the Governor wanted confirmation that the ships were a threat before he mobilized any troops. Jefferson sent General Thomas Nelson to the region to investigate, and, *"take such measures as exigencies may require."*[1]

When two days passed without further word, Jefferson concluded that the report was a false alarm. On January 2nd, however, he was shocked to learn that a strong British force had entered the James River.

Benedict Arnold's 1,200 man expedition included German jagers (riflemen), mounted Rangers, the 80th British Regiment, and a regiment of loyalists.[2] Arnold's mission was to disrupt Virginia's war effort and reduce the state's aid to General Nathanael Greene's army in the Carolinas.[3]

---

[1] Boyd, "Thomas Jefferson to General Steuben, 31 December, 1780," *The Papers of Thomas Jefferson, Vol. 4,* 254

[2] Johann Ewald, *Diary of the American War: A Hessian Journal,* (New Haven and London: Yale University Press, 1979), 266

[3] Selby, 222

Governor Jefferson scrambled to respond to Arnold's arrival. He informed General Nelson that,

> *Orders go out by the members of the Assembly to call together Half the Militia of the most convenient Counties...and one fourth from more distant Counties. We mean to have four thousand six hundred Militia in the Field.*[4]

Jefferson's hopes were severely hampered by the sluggish response of war weary Virginians. Less than a hundred men assembled at Hood's Point, an important artillery position overlooking the James River.[5] On January 3rd, they weakly challenged Arnold's approach, firing a few shots before fleeing.[6] Arnold continued upriver and landed at Westover Plantation the next day. On the evening of January 4th, he led his troops overland to Richmond. They arrived outside Virginia's capital the next afternoon and brushed aside the local militia. Public stores and buildings, as well as a few private dwellings, were pillaged and destroyed. An important foundry outside of Richmond was also severely damaged.[7]

On January 6th, Arnold sent over forty boats loaded with plunder down the James River and marched the rest of his force back to Westover.[8] Arnold was eager to return to the protection of his transport ships before Virginia's militia grew too strong. Captain Johann Ewald of the Jagers recalled that sixty men, fatigued by the rapid pace of the march, straggled behind and fell into American hands.[9]

---

[4] Boyd, "Thomas Jefferson to Thomas Nelson, 2 January, 1781," *The Papers of Thomas Jefferson, Vol. 4,* 297

[5] Boyd, "Arnold's Invasion as Reported by Jefferson in the Virginia Gazette, 13 January, 1781," *The Papers of Thomas Jefferson, Vol. 4,* 269

[6] Ewald, 261

[7] Boyd, " Arnold's Invasion as Reported by Jefferson...," *The Papers of Thomas Jefferson, Vol. 4,* 269

[8] Ewald, 268

[9] Ibid.

Virginia 1781

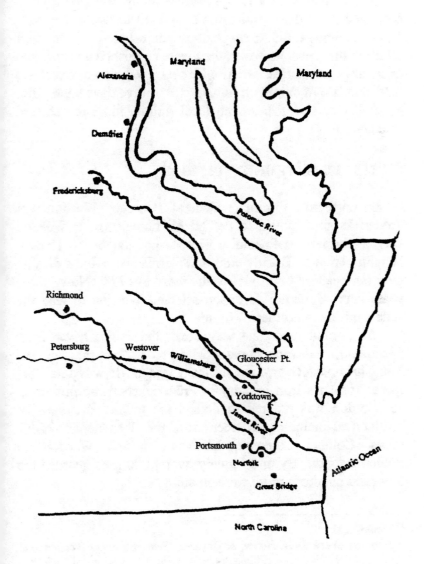

Arnold reached Westover and the protection of his ships on January 7th. He remained there until January 10th, when his troops boarded the transports and continued down river.

Reports that militia troops were waiting at Hood's Point prompted Arnold to send a force by land to attack the post. The detachment found the battery unoccupied. On their return to the ships, however, they were ambushed and suffered over forty casualties.[10] Arnold continued down river and landed at Isle of Wight on January 15th. Five days later, after a number of skirmishes with local militia, his force entered Portsmouth.

Northern Virginia Alarmed

In northern Virginia, General George Weedon, of Fredericksburg, moved to defend his hometown.[11] Weedon was a former continental officer who fought at Harlem Heights, Trenton, Brandywine, and Germantown, but a dispute over rank caused him to leave the army in 1778. Now, three years later, Governor Jefferson selected Weedon to lead the state's militia in northern Virginia.

As Arnold made his way down the James River from Richmond, concern spread that Fredericksburg, via the Rappahannock River, was his next target. It was vital that James Hunter's iron foundry in Fredericksburg be protected, so Weedon was ordered to defend the town. Hundreds of militiamen, including riflemen from the Shenandoah Valley under Colonel Sampson Mathews, joined Weedon in Fredericksburg. By mid-January over 1,000 men guarded the town and hundreds more were on alert.[12]

---

[10] Ewald, 271

[11] Harry M. Ward, *Duty, Honor, or Country: General George Weedon and the American Revolution*, (Philadelphia: American Philosophical Society, 1979), 63

[12] Ibid., 164

With Virginia's militia thoroughly alarmed, Arnold was reluctant to leave the safety of his earthworks and naval support in Portsmouth. This allowed the crisis to abate to the point that Virginia officials resumed their assistance to General Greene's army in North Carolina. Jefferson ordered a thousand militia troops to join General Greene on February 15th. A thousand more militiamen from northern Virginia were called into service to replace those going south:[13]

> *To the County Lieutenants of Loudoun, Fairfax, Prince William, and Fauquier.*
>
> *You will be pleased immediately on receipt of this, to order one fourth of your Militia to be assembled and marched without delay to Wmsburg...Send as many riflemen among them with their rifles as can be had, and of the rest let every man bring a good musket and accoutrements who has one. Let them proceed first to Fredericksburg where we shall endeavour to have such armed as bring no Arms of their own; from thence they must proceed to Wmsburg....*[14]

Unfortunately, the counties were slow to respond to this directive. In early March, Weedon sheepishly informed Governor Jefferson that he was still in Fredericksburg awaiting troops from Fauquier and Loudoun Counties. Jefferson urged Weedon to hurry on to Williamsburg:

> *For God's sake lose not a moment (indeed I am sure you will not) in getting on. Every instant is critical and may have great effect on operations.*[15]

[13] Ward, 174

[14] Boyd, "To the County Lieutenants of Loudoun, Fairfax, Prince William, and Fauquier, 17 February, 1781," *The Papers of Thomas Jefferson, Vol. 4*, 636-637

[15] Boyd, "Thomas Jefferson to George Weedon, 5 March, 1781," *The Papers of Thomas Jefferson, Vol. 5*, 71

The operations that Jefferson referred to were an assault on Portsmouth. The recent appearance of a French naval squadron off the Virginia Capes severed Arnold's access to the sea and trapped him in Portsmouth. With the impending arrival of continental reinforcements under the Marquis de LaFayette, Governor Jefferson saw an opportunity to capture Arnold and his force. Jefferson wanted Weedon's men in Williamsburg as soon as possible to help tighten the noose.

General Weedon heeded Jefferson's plea and immediately marched to Williamsburg. On March 9th, he reported to Jefferson from Hanover Courthouse:

> *I have reason to believe P. William and Fairfax will send forward their full Quota...In consequence of the disappointment from Loudoun, have been able to put Musquets in the hand of all those on the march. Some cartouch boxes and Bayonetts are wanting to Compleat them for Service which I am in hopes may be got below...The Troops are also furnished with a Camp Kettle to every 8 men and two Axes to each Company, upon the whole they are tolerable Equipt, all to Covering.*[16]

A day later, when he arrived in Williamsburg, Weedon's optimistic tone soured:

> *The deranged situation of our defence in this Quarter makes it absolutely necessary more Men should be call'd from above. I find from Baron de Steuben's situation, that the Militia in the neighbouring Counties are more backward than I could at this Time of alarm [have] expected.*[17]

---

[16] Boyd, "Jefferson to Weedon, 9 March, 1781," *The Papers of Thomas Jefferson, Vol. 5*, 109

[17] Boyd, "Weedon to Jefferson, 10 March, 1781," *The Papers of Thomas Jefferson, Vol. 5*, 122

General Weedon delivered more bad news to Governor Jefferson on March 21st. A new squadron of ships off the Virginia Capes that was originally believed to be French was in fact British![18] The ships were part of a 2,500 man British relief expedition under General William Phillips. Their arrival marked an end to the planned American assault on Portsmouth.[19] It was time for the British to resume the offensive and the Potomac River was one of their targets.

Potomac Raids

Reports that British ships were in the Potomac reached Governor Jefferson in early April. Edmund Reed, of Caroline County, forwarded news to Jefferson from King George County:

> *There was two large Sloops and three Small Vessells of the Enemy...* [who] *landed on the Maryland Shore* [and] *did Considerable* [mischief], *they then Crossed the River and Landed at Mr. Hooes and burnt down his Houses last evening, taken off Negroes, Stock, etc.*[20]

Three days later Read updated Jefferson with an eyewitness account:

> *The whole of the fleete amounted to two twenty four Gun Ships, two Eighteen* [gun ships] *and Six Transports and Tenders. They seem to be crowded with men.*[21]

---

[18] Boyd, "Weedon to Jefferson, 21 March, 1781," *The Papers of Thomas Jefferson, Vol. 5*, 203

[19] Ward, 269

[20] Boyd, "Edmund Read to Thomas Jefferson, 7 April, 1781," *The Papers of Thomas Jefferson, Vol. 5*, 371

[21] Boyd, "Edmund Read to Thomas Jefferson, 10 April, 1781," *The Papers of Thomas Jefferson, Vol. 5*, 399

Read speculated that Alexandria was their objective.[22] He was apparently unaware that a British privateer visited the town ten days earlier. Henry Lee II gave Jefferson a detailed account of the visit:

On the first [of April] *a Small Schoner...tender to the* [British] *privateer Trimer...with 21 Men...went up to Alexandria and in the Night Attempted to Cut out before the town a Vessel belonging to Baltimore. Fortunately they were discovered and the wind Changing prevented their Succeeding. They immediately made off down the river and were pursued by two Armed Vessels and...was taken before they got to the Trimer which with the Supprise and another Sloop of War laid at Cedar point...As soon as the Schoner found she Must be taken the Men took to their boats and landed on the Virginia Side of the River.*[23]

Lee reported that sixteen men were captured by local inhabitants. Half of the captured men were sent to Fredericksburg and the other half were sent to Alexandria. Colonel Lee informed Jefferson that when he learned that more British ships were sailing upriver he

Ordered all the [Prince William County] *Militia that Could be Armed to rendezvous at the Mouth of Quantico and there have been these two days about forty there on duty.*[24]

---

[22] Ibid.

[23] Boyd, "Henry Lee Sr. to Thomas Jefferson, 10 April, 1781," *The Papers of Thomas Jefferson, Vol. 5,* 393-94

[24] Ibid.

Colonel Lee also revealed disturbing information gleaned from the captured British sailors:

> *If the Enemy had Succeeded at Alexandria they intended; one of the Prisoners say, to have burnt General Washingtons Houses, Plundered Colo. Mason and myself and endeavoured to have made me a prisoner.*[25]

Fortunately for Colonel Mason and Colonel Lee, their property was untouched. General Washington was not so lucky. A number of his slaves were taken by a British raider. Lund Washington went aboard the ship and provided refreshments and provisions in an attempt to gain the return of the slaves and protect General Washington's property. Washington's buildings were spared, but his slaves were not returned. When General Washington learned of his cousin's actions, he immediately wrote and scolded him:

> *I am very sorry to hear of your loss; I am a little sorry to hear of my own; but which gives me most concern, is, that you should go on board the enemys Vessels, and furnish them with refreshments. It would have been a less painful circumstance to me, to have heard, that in consequence of your non-compliance with their request, they had burnt my House, and laid the Plantation in ruins. You ought to have considered yourself as my representative, and should have reflected on the bad example of communicating with the enemy, and making a voluntary offer of refreshments to them with a view to prevent a conflagration...But to go on board their Vessels; carry them refreshments; commune with a parcel of plundering Scoundrels, and request a favor by asking the surrender of my Negroes, was*

---

[25] Ibid.

exceedingly ill-judged, and 'tis to be feared, will be unhappy in its consequences, as it will be a precedent for others...Unless a stop to [the British raids occurs], I have little doubt of its ending in the loss of all my Negroes, and in the destruction of my Houses; but I am prepared for the event....[26]

Fortunately for Washington and the rest of northern Virginia, the British left the Potomac in late April. General Weedon informed Governor Jefferson of their withdrawal on April 21st:

Getting Intelligence of the Ships coming down [river, I] proceeded to Hollis's marsh where a body of Militia ware drawn together under the command of Colo. Richard Henry Lee...As they [the ships] came down they landed at Joetank, took off several...Negroes and did other damage, again they landed at Mr. Hooes Ferry, distroy'd Mr. Hooes Furniture, broak his Windows, and set his House on fire, which was happily Extinguished. They are now all gone down.[27]

[26]John C. Fitzpatrick, "George Washington to Lund Washington, 30 April, 1781," *The Writings of George Washington, Vol. 22*, 14-15

[27] Boyd, "George Weedon to Thomas Jefferson, 21 April, 1781," *The Papers of Thomas Jefferson, Vol. 5*, 529

Petersburg

The Potomac raids were only a prelude to a much larger British offensive. In mid April, General Phillips and the bulk of his force, approximately 2,500 strong, sailed up the James River. They raided Williamsburg and destroyed the Virginia State naval docks on the Chickahominy River. On April 24th, they landed at City Point and marched west towards Petersburg to seize a cache of American military supplies.

Approximately 1,000 militia, under Generals Muhlenberg and Steuben, waited for the British at Petersburg. Both men were experienced commanders and realized that their force was too weak to stop the British. They hoped to at least make General Phillips pay a price for the town. The Virginians formed two separate lines east of Petersburg. The first extended along a ridge on the edge of the village of Blandford. The second was situated about half a mile back, behind a wide marshy area on the edge of Petersburg. [28]

General Phillips approached Blandford around 2:00 p.m. on April 25th. His plan of attack was simple. Since he significantly outnumbered the Americans, he extended his line past the American right flank and ordered a frontal assault. Phillips instructed his left wing to turn the American right flank and push them towards the river.

Although they were greatly outnumbered, the first militia line held its ground for thirty minutes. [29] The second line was even more determined in its stand. Private George Connolly claimed that he fired twenty-three rounds (virtually an entire cartridge box), before wounds forced him to retire. [30] Over the span of an hour, two British charges were repelled. General Phillips finally used his cannon to break the Virginians and

---

[28] Robert Davis, *The Revolutionary War: The Battle of Petersburg*, E. & R. Davis, 2002, 11

[29] Ibid., 18

[30] Ibid., 20

drive them across the Appomattox River. The militia destroyed the bridge behind them and scurried up a ridge to get out of range of the British artillery. Victory belonged to the British, but Steuben's and Muhlenberg's men withdrew with the satisfaction that they fought well.

General Phillips followed his success at Petersburg with raids on an American supply depot at Chesterfield Court House and on the Virginia State Navy at Osborne Point. Both sites were destroyed. Phillips then turned his attention to Richmond. His troops entered Manchester, a village directly across the James River from Richmond, on April 29th. General Stueben, with the Virginia militia, and newly arrived General LaFayette, with 1,200 battle tested continental light infantry troops, were waiting for General Phillips in Richmond. The continentals arrived only a few hours ahead of the British and their presence altered General Phillip's plans.

He chose to avoid a fight with LaFayette and proceeded down the James River. On May 7th, Phillips received orders from General Cornwallis to return to Petersburg and rendezvous with the remnants of Cornwallis's force. After months of frustration in the Carolina's, General Cornwallis redirected his efforts in Virginia. His battered army of 1,500 men arrived in Petersburg on May 20th. Cornwallis assumed command of all British troops in Virginia. This included a recent reinforcement from New York that brought the total force to over 7,000 men.[31] General Cornwallis was deprived, however, of a key subordinate and friend. A few days before Cornwallis arrived in Petersburg, General Phillips succumbed to an illness and died.

---

[31] Selby, 275

Cornwallis vs. LaFayette

The arrival of Cornwallis created a very powerful British presence in the state, one that General LaFayette, the ranking American commander in Virginia, wished to avoid. LaFayette anxiously waited for his own reinforcements which consisted of over a thousand Pennsylvania continentals under General Anthony Wayne. Their march south was delayed by transport, supply, and discipline problems. LaFayette wanted no part of Cornwallis until Wayne's troops joined him.

As a result, the Americans retreated northward when the British crossed the James River on May 24th. It was the beginning of a ten day pursuit that saw both armies crisscross central Virginia.

In northern Virginia, concern about a visit from General Cornwallis was high. Hunter's iron foundry in Fredericksburg remained a likely target, and General George Weedon was once again charged with protecting it. When General Cornwallis's pursuit of LaFayette neared Fredericksburg, Weedon scrambled to organize the militia and remove military stores from the town.[32] Prince William County militiamen marched to Falmouth and joined troops from Stafford, Spottsylvania, and King George Counties.[33] William Brewer, of Prince William County, recalled that,

In June 1781 a draft was ordered in Prince William County for forty days. They rendezvoused at Dumfries and were to oppose the progress of Cornwallis' army which was marching through Virginia. They marched under Lt. Henry Lee, Capt.

---

[32] Ward, 194-195
[33] Ibid., 195

*Peyton, Maj. Ewell and Col. Ewell to Falmouth
where they united with Gen. Weedon's brigade.*[34]

Fortunately for General Weedon, who struggled to keep his troops in the field, General Cornwallis tired of his pursuit of LaFayette and spared Fredericksburg.[35] He redirected his attention to central Virginia.

In early June, two British detachments raided Charlottesville and Point of Fork. Lieutenant Colonel Banastre Tarleton's British Legion disrupted the Virginia Assembly and nearly captured Governor Jefferson in Charlottesville. Lieutenant Colonel James Simcoe was even more successful at Point of Fork. Although he was outnumbered almost three to one, Simcoe was able to disperse nearly 500 new Virginia continentals and destroy a large cache of military supplies. A few days after the raids, the two detachments re-united with General Cornwallis near Richmond. In mid June, the British slowly made their way to Williamsburg.

Cornwallis's march to Williamsburg allowed most of the counties in northern Virginia to discharge their militia.[36] William Brewer's company was an exception. It joined General LaFayette's army and followed Cornwallis south. LaFayette kept his distance from the British and waited for a chance to strike. An opportunity emerged in late June.

---

[34] Dorman, "William Brewer Pension Application," *Virginia Revolutionary Pension Applications, Vol. 10,* 18-19
[35] Ward, 195
[36] Ibid., 203

Spencer's Ordinary

On June 24th, Lieutenant Colonel John Simcoe led his corps of Queen's Rangers and a detachment of Jaegers on a patrol north of Williamsburg to destroy rebel boats and military stores near the Chickahominy River. Although they never located the boats, they discovered a number of cattle and provisions. They started back to Williamsburg late the next day and marched through the night. On the morning of June 26th, Simcoe stopped to rest his troops at Spencer's Ordinary, about six miles north of Williamsburg.

Unbeknownst to Simcoe, a large American detachment under Colonel Richard Butler of Pennsylvania marched all night to intercept Simcoe before he reached Williamsburg. Butler's force included a regiment of Pennsylvania continentals, two contingents of Virginia riflemen, and about 120 cavalry under Major William McPherson.[37] The horsemen rode ahead of Butler's infantry and surprised Simcoe's pickets around mid-morning. Major McPherson's horsemen charged through the British pickets, but they were repulsed by Simcoe's cavalry. McPherson was unhorsed and his men scattered. Fortunately for them, the riflemen and continental troops trotted onto the scene.

Although they were surprised and outnumbered by the Americans, Simcoe's men held firm. Captain Johann Ewald sent his Jaeger detachment around the American left flank to strike their rear. Ewald then led part of Simcoe's corps in a frontal assault upon the Americans:

---

[37] Hugh F. Rankin, *The War of the Revolution in Virginia*, (Williamsburg, VA: Virginia Independence Bicentennial Commission, 1979), 44

I called to Lieutenant Bickell to...fall upon the enemy's left flank and rear with all the jagers. At that instant, I jumped off my horse and placed myself in front of the center of the grenadiers and light infantry company. I asked them not to fire a shot, but to attack with the bayonet...The enemy...was taken aback by our advance. [They] *waited for us up to forty paces, fired a volley, killed two thirds of the grenadiers, and withdrew...We came among them and engaged them hand to hand. The enemy now came under rifle fire from the jagers on his flank and rear, and hurried to escape. We captured a French officer, a captain of riflemen, and twenty-two men, partly from the so-called Wild Irish Riflemen, and partly from the light infantry.*[38]

Ewald's attack was assisted by the actions of Lieutenant Colonel Simcoe and his cavalry. The American line was split by a road bordered by a sturdy fence. When the American troops on the right of the road saw Captain Ewald advance towards their comrades on the left, they scaled the fence to strike Ewald's left flank. This movement momentarily disordered the Americans and presented Simcoe's cavalry with the perfect opportunity to strike:

[The rebels] *did not observe the cavalry, which while they were in this disorder, lost not the moment, but...charged them up the road, and upon its left, entirely broke and totally dispersed them.*[39]

---

[38] Ewald, 309

[39] John G. Simcoe, *Simcoe's Military Journal: A History of the Operations of a Partisan Corps Called The Queen's Rangers*, (NY: Bartlett & Welford, 1844), 232

The entire American line fell back into some woods. Captain Ewald pursued but ended the chase when rebel reinforcements appeared. With his baggage and cattle safely en route to Williamsburg, Colonel Simcoe disengaged and resumed his march to town.

Green Spring

The British occupied Williamsburg for over a week while the Americans hovered nearby at New Kent Court House. On July 4th, Cornwallis broke camp and marched to Jamestown to cross the James River. His destination was Portsmouth. Before he crossed the river, however, Cornwallis set a trap for General LaFayette. He sent his baggage, as well as Simcoe's Corps, across the James and hid the rest of his troops along the shoreline. Pickets were placed on the road to Green Spring, a plantation two miles away. Cornwallis hoped to convince LaFayette that only his rearguard remained on the northern side of the river. He instructed his pickets to draw the Americans towards Jamestown, and the trap.

General Wayne took the bait on July 6th, and marched his 500 man advance guard towards Jamestown. His force included militia horsemen, Virginia riflemen, and Pennsylvania continentals. The Americans skirmished with British pickets and slowly advanced along a wooded causeway. General Wayne recalled:

> *At three o' clock the riflemen, supported by a few regulars, began and kept up a galling fire upon the enemy, which continued until five....*[40]

---

[40] Jared Sparks, ed. " Brigadier-General Wayne to General Washington, 8 July, 1781," *Correspondence of the American Revolution Being Letters of Eminent Men to George Washington,* (Boston: Little, Brown, and Co., 1853), 348
(Henceforth referred to as Wayne)

Lieutenant Colonel James Mercer, of Fredericksburg, commanded about 150 Virginia riflemen on the right flank of the American line. After a long running skirmish, the riflemen encountered a strong British detachment posted at a house. Mercer recalled:

> *The* [enemy] *Picket was speedily driven* [from a house] *with loss, & possession gain'd of the house. To support them & regain the house,* [a second British detachment] *advanc'd with spirit, but they were unable to stand the deadly fire of the Riflemen, and were driven back with...loss.... Tthe Riflemen embolden'd by this success, were with difficulty restrain'd from advancing...and a number of them crowded into the house and began to fire to the left on the main body of the British army now plainly discover'd at a distance of about 300 yards.*[41]

In the American center, General Wayne was startled by the sudden appearance of five British columns in his front. He *"Thought proper to order Major Galvan, at the head of the advanced guard, to meet and attack their front...."*[42] Galvan's 150 light infantrymen conducted a *"spirited though unequal,"* fight and withdrew after only a few minutes.[43]

Colonel Mercer witnessed Galvan's brave stand but was soon occupied with his own front. British artillery killed his horse and panicked his riflemen. Mercer recalled that as the riflemen scurried to the rear, *"The whole front line of the enemy was advancing with shouts."*[44] The situation was

---

[41] Gillard Hunt, ed., "Colonel John Francis Mercer," *Eyewitness Accounts of the American Revolution: Fragments of Revolutionary History,* (NY Times & Arno Press, Reprint, 1971), 48
(Originally printed in 1892 and henceforth referred to as Mercer)
[42] Wayne, 348
[43] Ibid.
[44] Mercer, 49

equally desperate on the American left, which quickly collapsed.

In the center, General Wayne struggled to make a stand. He was reinforced by two battalions of Pennsylvania continentals and a battalion of light infantry, but his 800 man line was still greatly outnumbered.[45] With the enemy pressing his flanks and threatening his rear, Wayne made a bold decision:

> *It was determined among a choice of difficulties, to advance and charge them. This was done with such vivacity as to produce the desired effect, that is, checking them in their advance, and diverting them from their* [attempted encirclement].[46]

Lieutenant William Feltman, a Pennsylvania continental, described the advance:

> *We...displayed to the right and left, the 3rd battalion on our right, and the 2nd on our left, being then formed,* [we] *brought on a general engagement, our advance* [was] *regular at a charge till we got within eighty yards of their whole army, they being regularly formed, standing one yard distance from each other...We advanced under a heavy fire of grape-shot at which distance we opened our musketry.*[47]

British Lieutenant Colonel Banastre Tarleton was impressed by the intensity of the fight:

---

[45] Rankin, 55

[46] Wayne, 348

[47] Peter Decher, ed., *Journal of Lt. William Feltman of the First Pennsylvania Regiment, 1781-1782,* (Samen, NH: Ayer Co, 1969),

> *The conflict in this quarter was severe and well*
> *contested.   The artillery and infantry of each*
> *army...were for some minutes warmly engaged not*
> *fifty yards asunder...on the left of the British, the*
> *action was for some time gallantly maintained by the*
> *continental infantry.* [48]

General Wayne's aggressiveness surprised the British and disrupted their attack.   This allowed the Americans to withdraw, albeit rather disorderly, and escape annihilation. Darkness assisted the Americans by preventing a British pursuit.

Although the battle was a clear British victory, American losses, which totaled approximately 140 men, could have been far worse.[49]   In that sense, the battle of Green Spring was a missed opportunity, one that General Cornwallis would soon regret.

Cornwallis moved his army to Portsmouth and stayed there through July.   LaFayette remained on the northern bank of the James River and waited.   In early August, Cornwallis sailed to Yorktown and fortified the town.   This presented the Americans with an unexpected opportunity.   General Washington, with the main American army outside of New York, had planned for months to attack New York with a combined French-American force.   The proposed assault required the coordination of French land and sea forces, however, something that proved difficult to accomplish.

---

[48] Banastre Tarleton, *A History of the Campaigns of 1780 and 1781 in the Southern Provinces of North America,* (North Stratford, NH: Ayer Co., Reprinted, 1999), 354
(Originally printed in 1787)
[49] Henry P. Johnson, *The Yorktown Campaign and the Surrender of Cornwallis: 1781,* (Eastern National, 1997), 190
(Originally printed in 1881)

Bagging Cornwallis

The news of Cornwallis's move to Yorktown reached Washington on the heels of news that a large French naval squadron planned to sail to the Chesapeake Bay and remain until October. This created an ideal opportunity to sever Cornwallis's supply line to New York. If General Washington, in conjunction with the French, could position enough troops in Virginia to besiege Cornwallis at Yorktown, they might be able to capture his entire army. Washington revealed his plans to various state leaders on August 21st:

> *The Fleet of the Count de Grasse, with a Body of French Troops on Board, will make its first Appearance in the Chesapeake… and should the Enemy under Lord Cornwallis hold their present Position in Virginia will give us the fairest Opportunity to reduce the whole British Force in the South, and to ruin their boasted Expectations in the Quarter: to effect this desirable Object, it has been judged expedient…to abandon the Seige of [New York] and to march a Body of Troops, consisting of a Detachment from the American Army, with the whole of the French Troops, immediately to Virginia. With this Detachment, which will be very considerable, I have determined to march myself. The American Troops are already on the West Side of the Hudson, and the French Army will arrive at Kings Ferry this Day.[50]*

The American and French troops rapidly marched south and boarded ships at the head of Chesapeake Bay. General Washington continued south by land in order to stop at Mount Vernon. He had been away from home for six years and

---

[50] Fitzpatrick, "Circular to the States, 21 August, 1781," *The Writing of George Washington, Vol. 22*, 26-27

returned on September 9th to a joyous reception. While he was eager to enjoy his visit and entertain his fellow officers, military considerations demanded his attention. Much of the army's baggage and equipment was transported overland and Washington was concerned that the condition of Virginia's roads would delay their progress. He, therefore, requested the County Lieutenant of Fairfax to use the militia for road repair rather than military service in Yorktown:

> *Instead of having the Militia of this County, (who I am informed are now assembled) march immediately to join the Marquis de la Fayette; I could wish they might be employed in repairing the Roads from George Town to the Ford of Occoquan. To do this without a moments loss of time is of such essential importance that I cannot but repeat in the most earnest manner my desire to have it done. The Waggons of the French and American Armies, the Cavalry, and the Cattle will proceed by that rout and may be expected in a few days; and will not only be retarded but more than probably essentially injured, if this necessary business is neglected or delayed. I depend therefore absolutely upon your zeal and activity for the execution of this business.*[51]

Henry Lee II, the County Lieutenant of Prince William County, received a similar request. His men repaired the road from Occoquon Ford to Dumfries. General Washington asked a little extra from the gentlemen of Prince William County; he wanted carriages to transport the French officers to Fredericksburg.

---

[51] Fitzpatrick, "General Washington to Peter Waggoner, 9 September, 1781, The Writings of George Washington, Vol. 23, 109

I expect Count de Rochambeau (Commander of the French Army) the Chevlr. De Chastellux & their respective suite at this place [Mount Vernon] tomorrow on their way to join the army below. It would be a relief to them & their horses, and a mark of attention w'ch I am persuaded would be pleasing [to] the Gentlemen, if this State would assist them along in their carriages from stage to stage. Permit me therefore to request the favour of you to provide at Dumfries the means of carrying them to Fredericksburg, where I will engage other Gentlemen to take them up, from hence they will be furnished with carriages & horses to Dumfries.[52]

Colonel Lee complied with Washington's request and informed Virginia officials of his action:

I draughted one half of my Militia amounting to 285 privates...and had them ready last Wednesday, to march, but in consequence of his Excellency Genl: Washington's [letter]...I have kept them on severe Duty in repairing the roads wch: were impassable for the Baggage Waggons and Artillery, which has been a laborious & fatiguing Duty—I saw his Excellency as he passed through Dumfries last Wednesday, who directed me, in conjunction with Colo. Wagener...to view and Examine the Ford of Occoquon at a place called Wolfe-run-ford, and if it was Possible, to make the hills there, which were by nature inaccessible, a way for waggons, to have it done...the way was viewed and found might be made a good road with much labour, and half of my Militia, draughts and

---

[52] William Palmer, "General Washington to Henry Lee Sr., 10 September, 1781," *Calendar of Virginia State Papers, Vol. 2*, (Richmond: James E. Goode, 1881), 452-453

all, are & have been Employed about that work, and in a few days I am in hopes will be completely accomplished, w'ch will open a direct way from Georgetown to Dumfries and shorten the distance many miles besides being a much better road, and well supplied with forage.... The Genl: likewise advised me not to send the militia to head Quarters until I heard from him or the Governour...Pray inform the Gov'r of the reason this Militia has not marched [to Yorktown].[53]

It was fortunate that the Prince William militia was not sent south for they were desperately short of arms. Lee noted that,

We have not above 80 guns in the County that are anywise fit for Service and about as many Squerill Guns.[54]

The road work, which caused most of the militia from Prince William and Fairfax Counties to miss the siege of Yorktown, was not the only task assigned northern Virginia leaders. Washington's army was in desperate need of flour, and the counties of northern Virginia were urged to send what they could. Colonel James Hendricks, of Fairfax County, scrambled to obtain provisions for the troops. He quickly grew frustrated and complained to a state official about the lack of effort from the other counties:

I lament the want of vigorous Exertions in your Assistants in the Counties above me – yesterday came three wagons (which I had impressed in Loudoun) without any flour. I now have it in my Power to send by water all the flour that is made in Fairfax,

---

[53] Palmer, "Col: Henry Lee to Col: Davies, 17 September, 1781 ," *Calendar of Virginia State Papers, Vol. 2,* 451-452
[54] Ibid., 452

Loudon, Berkely, Frederick, Hampshire, &
Shenandoah, if it was order'd here.[55]

A few days later, Hendricks implored leaders in Berkely
County to send all the flour they could spare:

> *For God's sake exert yourself and send down all the*
> *Flour you can, as our Army is in a starving condition*
> *– let the People know that this is in all probability the*
> *last time they will be call'd on in this manner – a few*
> *weeks exertions and the enemy is expelled* [from] *our*
> *State forever.*[56]

Events soon transpired in Yorktown to fulfill this
prediction.

Gloucester Point

There were actually two British encampments in the
vicinity of Yorktown. The bulk of Cornwallis's army was
posted behind strong earthworks in the town itself. A separate
detachment held a fortified position across the York River at
Gloucester Point. For most of September, American troops
kept a safe distance from both camps. General LaFayette was
posted in Williamsburg, and General George Weedon
commanded a detachment of militia about ten miles above
Gloucester Point. Weedon's detachment numbered around
1,200 men and included hundreds of Loudoun County
militia.[57] A company of militia from Prince William County
joined Weedon after it completed the road repairs up north.[58]

---

[55] Palmer, "James Hendricks to John Pierce, Esqr., 21 September, 1781,"
Calendar of Virginia State Papers, Vol. 2, 478
[56] Palmer, "Col: James Hendricks to James McAlister of Berkely Co., 26
September, 1781," *Calendar of Virginia State Papers, Vol. 2,* 495
[57] Ward, 216-217; and Dorman, the Revolutionary War Pension
Applications of:
 Samuel Conn, *Virginia Revolutionary Pension Applications*, Vol. 21,

General Weedon was reinforced in late September by 600 French troops under General Lauzun. Half of the French reinforcements were cavalry and the other half were infantry. A few days later, 800 French Marines, under General Choisy, joined Weedon. The influx of French troops prompted General Cornwallis to send Banastre Tarleton and a thousand men across the river to bolster the post at Gloucester Point. The next day, a large British foraging party clashed with a combined force of French cavalry and Virginia militia.

The battle began when a detachment of militia cavalry encountered the British rear guard under Tarleton.[59] Generals Choisy and Lauzun rushed their cavalry to the scene. When they arrived, Colonel Tarleton attacked them with his own cavalry. He recalled that,

> *The whole of the English rear guard set out full speed from its distant situation, and arrived in such disorder, that its charge was unable to make an impression on the Duke of Lauzun's hussars....*[60]

Tarleton was unhorsed but managed to escape in the meelee. When the French pursued the fleeing British, they ran into musket fire from British infantry in a thicket. Tarleton noted that,

84
Samual Beavers, *Virginia Revolutionary Pension Applications*, Vol. 5, 96
Thomas Bailey, *Virginia Revolutionary Pension Applications*, Vol. 3, 96
[58] Dorman, "John Burch Revolutionary War Pension Application," *Virginia Revolutionary Pension Applications*, Vol. 12, 89
[59] Tarleton, 376
[60] Ibid., 377

The fire of this party restrained the enemy's hussars, and the British were soon rallied. A disposition was instantly made to charge the front of the hussars with one hundred and fifty dragoons, whilst a detachment wheeled upon their flank: No shock, however, took place between the two bodies of cavalry; the French hussars retired behind their infantry and a numerous militia who had arrived at the edge of the plain.[61]

The infantry that Tarleton observed were 160 Virginia militia under Lieutenant Colonel James Mercer. They arrived on the scene just in time to see the French repulsed. Mercer recalled that his men *"were at first some what startled to find the French horse retreating so rapidly..."*[62] The Virginians recovered their nerve and deployed to meet the oncoming British. Mercer proudly recalled:

They...[formed] with great celerity & good order, & commenced firing, one half on the cavalry on the right, & the other half on the infantry advancing rapidly thro' the wood. The horse of the enemy had approach'd within 250 yards & the infantry were not at more than 150 yards distance when the firing began. No regular troops cou'd behave with more zeal & alacrity than this corps of Militia; their spirits had been rais'd by running them up, and being hurried into action without time to reflect on their danger, they discovered as much gallantry & order as any regular corps that I ever saw in action. Fortunately Tarleton did not like the reception prepared for him & at a critical moment sounded a retreat, when not 100 cartridges remain'd unexpended in the regiment....[63]

---

[61] Ibid., 377-378
[62] Mercer, 58
[63] Mercer, 59

Tarleton and his men returned to the safety of their fortifications, satisfied with the result of the forage. They were unaware that the skirmish marked the last time they would leave their fortifications at Gloucester Point.

Victory

Across the river, American and French forces steadily squeezed General Cornwallis and his troops. The allies arrived at Yorktown on September 28th and spent a week preparing for the siege. Construction of the first parallel (siege trench) began on October 6th. The Americans and French endured a steady bombardment and finally responded on October 9th with their own batteries. Soon, allied firepower surpassed the British, and Cornwallis's men suffered significantly. On October 11th, the allies began a second parallel only 400 yards from Yorktown. A daring night bayonet assault by French and American troops on two British outposts allowed the second parallel to be completed on October 15th.

Allied cannon now pounded Yorktown at point blank range. Cornwallis sent a 350 man sortie into the allied lines on October 16th, but they inflicted limited damage, and the allied bombardment of Yorktown continued. On October 17th, General Cornwallis asked for terms, and the garrison surrendered two days later.

Although America's victory at Yorktown essentially ended the war, months of negotiations occurred before it was officially over. In the meantime, America had thousands of new prisoners to attend to. Many were escorted north by members of the Loudoun County militia. They eventually arrived at Fort Frederick, Maryland.

This guard detail was the last military service of the war for the militia of Loudoun County. Like their comrades from Fairfax and Prince William, they returned home satisfied that they had helped expel the British from their soil.

America's long struggle with Britain officially ended in 1783. The former colonists of Great Britain were now a sovereign people. Few envisioned such a thing prior to 1775. Yet, the desire to preserve cherished rights prompted thousands of Americans to risk their lives in a noble struggle, and Virginians from Loudoun, Fairfax, and Prince William County led the way.

Appendix

Sites of Historical Interest

Dumfries

Dumfries was once a thriving tobacco port town along Quantico Creek, a tributary of the Potomac River. The creek formed an excellent, sheltered harbor that attracted many ships. By the 1760's, Dumfries was the center of Prince William County political, business, and social life. The town boasted a number of taverns, warehouses, a theatre, horse track, and the county courthouse. The courthouse disappeared long ago, but the lot, which overlooks southbound Route 1, remains. A small monument commemorating the 1774 Prince William County Resolves sits on the northwest corner of the lot, in the shadow of **Alexander Henderson's house**. A block away is the **Weems-Botts museum**, named after Parson Weems, a biographer of George Washington, and William Botts, a local lawyer. The building, like the Henderson house, is contemporary to the colonial period, as is **Williams Ordinary**, the large brick building that sits along southbound Route 1. Although the rest of the town is peppered with modern structures, the streets still lie on original roadbeds and a quick walk about town allows one to envision what Dumfries was like in its heyday.

Unfortunately years of tobacco cultivation led to massive soil erosion in the latter half of the 18th century. The harbor gradually clogged with silt and by the end of the 1790's the town of Dumfries had significantly declined.

Possum Point / Quantico Creek

A short drive along Possum Point Road in Dumfries provides an excellent view of the sheltered harbor of Quantico Creek. Virtually all of the area east of the northbound lanes of Route 1 was underwater in the 18th century and the area was a busy port. Be sure to drive all the way to Possum Point Power Plant to get a great view of the harbor and creek. Somewhere in the vicinity of the power plant, local militia troops built fortifications to protect Dumfries from British raids. Confederate soldiers did likewise in 1861 in an attempt to blockade the Potomac River.

Quantico Marine Base / Chopawamsic Creek

Chopawamsic Creek, the boundary between Prince William and Stafford county, enters the Potomac River near the Marine airfield at Quantico. Although the terrain has been extensively altered and developed, an excellent view of the Potomac River is attainable from the rear parking lot of the base gymnasium. Local militia troops fortified the mouth of Chopawamsic Creek in the vicinity of the gymnasium.

Leesylvania State Park

Viewed by many local residents as a recreational park for boating and picnics, Leesylvania is also a historic site. Henry Lee II, one of Prince William County's most important political leaders in the Revolution and the father of Light Horse Harry Lee, resided on the land. A historic trail leads to the house site, long destroyed, and Henry Lee's gravesite. The park also includes the remnants of a Confederate artillery battery overlooking the Potomac River as well as a fine visitor's center.

Rippon Lodge

Rippon Lodge was the home of Thomas Blackburn, a neighbor of Henry Lee II and another important political leader from Prince William County. The house sits on a wooded hill overlooking Neabsco Creek and is the oldest structure in Prince William County, dating to the 1740's. The county plans to restore the house and open it to the public.

Colchester

Once a thriving colonial town at the mouth of the Occoquan River in Fairfax County, Colchester has since disappeared, replaced by a boat marina. Old Colchester Road ends at the Occoquan River and lies on the original roadbed. One can imagine the busy ferry crossing and town along the bank of the river. Two houses from the period still remain. They are both located on the west side of the road.

Old Colchester Road

Present day Old Colchester Road largely follows the original roadbed from Colchester to Pohick Church on a wonderful, winding, road across Mason Neck in Fairfax County. The road is part of the Washington-Rochembeu Route to Yorktown.

Pohick Church

At the intersection of Old Colchester Road and Route 1 is Pohick Church. Completed in 1774 it included such parishioners as George Washington, George Mason, and William Fairfax. Pohick Church survived both the Revolutionary and Civil War and remains an active Episcopalian Church today.

Gunston Hall

Gunston Hall was the plantation of George Mason, considered by many to be one of Virginia's best legal minds. Mason was a delegate to a number of Revolutionary conventions and was the principle author of the Prince William and Fairfax Resolves, the Virginia Declaration of Rights, and Virginia's first constitution. His property encompassed a large portion of present day Mason Neck. Today, 550 acres of this property, along with his house, are open to the public as a museum. The site is managed by the state and includes an excellent Visitors Center and museum and numerous walking paths around the grounds.

Mount Vernon

Mount Vernon was the plantation home of George Washington. At one point it encompassed over 8,000 acres of the surrounding area. Today, the Mount Vernon Ladies Association manages over 500 acres, including the mansion and numerous outbuildings. The site is open year round and is one of the most visited sites in America.

Claude Moore Colonial Farm

This small living history site in Fairfax County provides an outstanding example of a tenant family's life in Virginia in the early 1770's. The staff interpret the site _"in character"_ and allow visitors to observe the workings of a small family farm.

Leesburg

Founded in 1758, Leesburg was the center of commerce for the rich agricultural lands of Loudoun County. Numerous 18th and 19th century buildings line the center of this colonial crossroads town.

Sites in Alexandria

Old Town Alexandria

Perched on the bank of the Potomac River, Alexandria was a bustling tobacco town and port during the Revolution. It served as a supply depot and hospital center in the war and was frequently occupied by militia troops for its defense. A number of 18th century buildings and cobblestone streets make a walk about Alexandria a very pleasurable experience.

Christ Church

Built in 1773, the church was attended by George Washington and many other prominent residents of Fairfax County.

Gadsby's Tavern

Although this building actually dates a few years after the Revolution, it is an outstanding site to visit to learn about life in the new country. Gadsby's Tavern hosted numerous dances, plays, musical performances, and political meetings in the 1780's and 1790's.

Carlyle House

Built in the early 1750's by one of Alexandria's founders, John Carlyle, the mansion is full of period furnishings. It stands as an example of the prosperity generated in the booming commercial port town of Alexandria.

Ramsay House

Built in the 18th century by one of Alexandria's founders, William Ramsey, the building now serves as the city's visitors center.

Bibliography

Abbot, W.W., and Dorothy Twohig. eds. *The Papers of George Washington: Colonial Series, Vol. 7.* Charlottesville: University Press of Virginia, 1990.

Ballagh, James C. ed., *Letters of Richard Henry Lee, Vol. 1.* New York : Macmillan Co., 1911.

Boatner III, Mark M. *Encyclopedia of the American Revolution.* 3rd ed., Stanpole Books, 1994.

Boyd, Julian. ed. *The Papers of Thomas Jefferson, Vol. 3-6.* Princeton, NJ: Princeton University Press, 1951.

Boyle, Joseph Lee. *Writings from the Valley Forge Encampment of the Continental Army.* Vol. 1-2 Bowie: Heritage Books Inc., 2000.

Buchanan, John. *The Road to Guilford Courthouse: The American Revolution in the Carolina.* NY: John Wiley & Sons, Inc., 1997.

Campbell, Charles. *The Orderly Book of that Portion of the American Army stationed at or near Williamsburg, Virginia under the command of General Andrew Lewis, from March 18th, 1776 to August 20th, 1776.* Richmond, VA: 1860.

Carrington, Henry B. *Battles of the American Revolution.* New York: A. S. Barnes & Co., 1877.

Cecere, Michael. *An Officer of Very Extraordinary Merit: Charles Porterfield and the American War for Independence, 1775-1780.* Westminster, MD: Heritage Books, 2004.

Cecere, Michael. *Captain Thomas Posey and the 7th Virginia Regiment.* Westminster, MD: Heritage Books, 2005.

Cecere, Michael. *They Behaved Like Soldiers: Captain John Chilton and the Third Virginia Regiment.* Westminster, MD: Heritage Books, 2004.

Chase, Philander D. ed. *The Papers of George Washington: Revolutionary War Series.* Charlottesville: University Press of Virginia, 2000.

Clark, William, ed. *Naval Documents of the American Revolution, Vol. 1-5.* Washington: 1970.

Commager, Henry Steele. *Documents of American History,* New York: Appleton-Century-Crofts, 1963.

Commager, Henry and Richard Morris, ed. *The Spirit of 'Seventy-Six: The Story of the American Revolution as Told by Participants.* NY: Castle Books, 1967.

Conrad, Dennis M. *The Papers of General Nathanael Greene, Vol. 9-11.* Chapel Hill: University of North Carolina Press, 1997-2000.

Cresswell, Nicholas. *The Journal of Nicholas Cresswell; 1774-1777.* New York: The Dial Press, 1924.

Cullen, Charles and Herbert Johnson, ed. *The Papers of John Marshall, Vol. 1.* Chapel Hill : Univ. of NC Press, 1974.

Dann, John C. *The Revolution Remembered: Eyewitness Accounts of the War Independence.* Chicago: University of Chicago Press, 1980.

Davis, Robert. *The Revolutionary War: The Battle of Petersburg.* E. & R. Davis, 2002.

Decher, Peter. ed., *Journal of Lt. William Feltman of the First Pennsylvania Regiment, 1781-1782.* Samen, NH: Ayer Co, 1969.

Dorman, John Frederick. *Virginia Revolutionary Pension Applications, Volumes 1-52.* Washington D.C., 1958-1995.

Draper, Lyman C. *King's Mountain and Its Heroes: History of the Battle of King's Mountain.* Cincinnati: Peter G. Thomson, 1881.

Ewald, Captain Johann. *Diary of the American War: A Hessian Journal.* New Haven: Yale Univ. Press, 1979. Translated & edited by Joseph Tustin.

Fischer, David Hackett. *Washington's Crossing.* Oxford University Press, 2004.

Fitzpatrick, John C. *The Writings of George Washington from the Original Manuscripts, 1745-1799.* Washington: U.S. Govt. Printing Office, 1931.

Force, Peter. ed., *American Archives: 5th Series.* Washington D.C.: U.S. Congress, 1848-1853.

Godwin, Mary. *Cloathing and Accoutrements of the Officers and Soldiers of the Virginia Forces: 1775-1788.* Unpublished, 1962.

Graham, James. *The Life of General Daniel Morgan.*
    Bloomingburg, NY: Zebrowski Historical Services,
    1993. Press of Virginia, 1965.

Hamilton, Stanislaus M. ed. *Letters to Washington &*
    Accompanying Papers, Vol. 5. Boston & New York:
    Houghton, Mifflin, Co., 1902.

Heckert, C.W. *A German-American Diary: Notes of Related*
    Historical Interest, Including Translated Excerpts
    from the Wiederholdt Diary. Parsons, WV : McClain
    Printing Co., 1980.

Hening, William W. *The Statutes at Large Being a Collection*
    of all the Laws of Virginia, Vol. 9. Richmond: J. & G.
    Cochran, 1821.

Hume, Ivor Noel. *1775: Another Part of the Field.*
    New York: Alfred A. Knopf, 1966.

Hunt, Gillard ed., *Eyewitness Accounts of the American*
    Revolution: Fragments of Revolutionary History. NY
    Times & Arno Press, Reprint, 1971.
    Originally printed in 1892.

Hunt, Gaillard. ed., *The Writings of James Madison, Vol. 1.*
    NY: G.P. Putnam's Sons, 1900.

Jackson, John W. *Valley Forge: Pinnacle of Courage.*
    Gettysburg, PA: Thomas Publications, 1992.

Johnson, Henry. *The Battle of Harlem Heights.* London:
    Macmillian, 1897.

Johnson, Henry P. *The Campaign of 1776 Around New York*
    and Brooklyn. New York: Da Capa Press, 1971.

Johnson, Henry P. *The Yorktown Campaign and the Surrender of Cornwallis:* 1781. Eastern National, 1997. Originally printed in 1881.

Kapp, Friedrich. *The Life of Frederick William von Steuben.* NY: Corner House Historical Publications, 1999. (Originally published in 1859)

Katcher, Philip. "They Behaved Like Soldiers: The Third Virginia Regiment at Harlem Heights," *Virginia Cavalcade, Vol. 26.* No. 2, Autumn 1976.

Lee, Charles. *The Lee Papers, Vol. 1.* Collections of the New York Historical Society, 1871.

Lee, Henry. *The Revolutionary War Memoirs of General Henry Lee.* New York: Da Capo Press, 1998. Originally Published in 1812.

Lesser, Charles H. ed. *The Sinews of Independence: Monthly Strength Reports of the Continental Army.* Chicago: The Univiversity of Chicago Press, 1976.

Marshall, John. *The Life of George Washington, Vol. 2.* Fredericksburg, VA: The Citizens Guild of Washington's Boyhood Home, 1926.

McILwaine, H. R. ed., *Journals of the Council of the State of Virginia, Vol. 1.* Richmond, 1931.

McMichael, James. "The Diary of Lt. James McMichael of the Pennsylvania Line, 1776-1778," *The Pennsylvania Magazine of History and Biography.* Vol. 16, no. 2, 1892.

Moore, Frank. *Diary of the American Revolution, from Newspapers and Original Documents.* 2 vols. New York:Charles Schibner, 1860. Reprint. New York: New York Times & Arno Press, 1969.

O'Kelly, Patrick. *Nothing But Blood and Slaughter: The Revolutionary War in the Carolinas.* Blue House Tavern Press, 2004.

Palmer, William. *Calendar of Virginia State Papers, Vol. 1- 2.* Richmond: James E. Goode, 1881.

Posey, John Thornton. *General Thomas Posey: Son of the American Revolution.* East Lansing: Michigan State Univ. Press, 1992.

Posey, Thomas. *A Short Biography of the Life of Governor Thomas Posey.* Thomas Posey Papers. Indiana Historical Society Library, Indianapolis, IN.

Posey, Thomas. *Revolutionary War Journal,* Thomas Posey Papers, Indiana Historical Society Library, Indianapolis, IN.

Powell, Robert. *Biographical Sketch of Col. Levin Powell, 1737-1810: Including his Correspondence during the Revolutionary War.* Alexandria, Virginia: G.H. Ramey & Son, 1877.

Rankin, Hugh F. *The War of the Revolution in Virginia.* Williamsburg, VA: Virginia Independence Bicentennial Commission, 1979.

Reed, John F. *Campaign to Valley Forge: July 1, 1777 – December 19, 1777.* Pioneer Press, 1980.

Rowland, Kate Mason. *The Life and Correspondence of George Mason, Vol. 1.* New York: Russell & Russell, 1964.

Rodney, Caesar. *The Diary of Captain Thomas Rodney, 1776-1777.* Wilmington: The Historical Society of Delaware, 1888.

Runge, Beverly. ed., *The Papers of George Washington: Colonial Series, Vol. 10.* Charlottesville, VA: University Press of Virginia, 1995.

Russell, T. Tripplett and John K. Gott, *Fauquier County in the Revolution,* Westminster, MD : Willow Bend Books, 1988.

Rutland, Robert A. ed., *The Papers of George Mason, Vol. 1.* University of North Carolina Press, 1970.

Ryan, Dennis P. *A Salute to Courage: The American Revolution as Seen Through Wartime Writings of Officers of the Continental Army and Navy.* NY: Columbia University Press, 1979.

Saffell, W.T.R. *Records of the Revolutionary War,* 3rd ed. Baltimore: Charles Saffell, 1894.

Sanchez-Saavedra, E.M. *A Guide to Virginia Military Organizations in the American Revolution, 1774-1787.* Westminster, MD: Willow Bend Books, 1978.

Scheer, George F., and Hugh F. Rankin. *Rebels & Redcoats: The American Revolution through the Eyes of Those Who Fought and Lived It.* New York: Da Capo Press, 1987.

Scribner, Robert L. and Tarter, Brent (comps). *Revolutionary Virginia: The Road to Independence, Volumes 1-7.* Charlottesville: University Press of Virginia, 1978.

Selby, John. *The Revolution in Virginia: 1775-1783.* Williamsburg, VA: The Colonial Williamsburg Foundation, 1988.

Sellers, John R. *The Virginia Continental Line.* Williamsburg: The Virginia Bicentennial Commission, 1978.

Sergeant R. "The Battle of Princeton," *The Pennsylvania Magazine of History and Biography, Vol. 20, No. 1.* 1896

Simcoe, Lt. Col. John. *Simcoe's Military Jouirnal: A History of the Operations of a Partisan Corps Called the Queen's Rangers, Commanded by Lieut. Col. J. G. Simcoe, During the War of Revolution.* New York: New York Times and Arno Press, 1968.

Smith, Samuel. *The Battle of Brandywine.* Monmouth Beach, NJ: Philip Freneau Press, 1976.

Smith, Samuel. *The Battle of Princeton.* Monmouth Beach, NJ: Philip Freneau Press, 1967.

Sparks, Jared. ed. *The Correspondence of the American Revolution being Letters of Eminent Men to George Washington, Vol. 2.* Boston : Little, Brown & Co., 1853.

Stryker, William. *The Battles of Trenton and Princeton.* Republished by The Old Barracks Association, Trenton NJ: 2001. (Originally published in 1898).

Symonds, Craig L. *A Battlefield ATLAS of the American Revolution.* The Nautical & Aviation Publishing Co. of America Inc., 1986.

Tarleton, Banastre. *A History of the Campaigns of 1780 and 1781 in the Southern Provinces of North America.* North Stratford, NH: Ayer Co., Reprinted, 1999 Originally printed in 1787.

Tarter, Brent and Robert Scribner. ed. *Revolutionary Virginia: The Road to Independence, Vol. 1-7.* University Press of Virginia, 1983.

Thacher, James. *A Military Journal during the American Revolutionary War.* Hartford: CT, S. Andrus and Son, 1854. Reprint, New York: Arno Press, 1969.

Tyler, Lyon. "The Old Virginia Line in the Middle States During the American Revolution," *Tyler's Quarterly Historical and Genealogical Magazine: Vol.12.* Richmond, VA: Richmond Press Inc., 1931.

Van Schreeven, William and Robert L. Scribner. ed., *Revolutionary Virginia: The Road to Independence, Vol. 1.* Charlottesville: University Press of Virginia, 1973.

Ward, Harry M. *Duty, Honor, or Country : General George Weedon and the American Revolution. Philadelphia :* American Philosophical Society, 1979.

Weedon, George. *Correspondence Account of the Battle of Brandywine, 11 September, 1777.* The original manuscript is in the collections of the Chicago Historical Society, Transcribed by Bob McDonald, 2001.

Wilkinson, James. *Memoirs of My Own Times, Vol. 1*
Philadelphia: Abraham Small, 1816
Reprinted by AMS Press Inc., : NY, 1973

Willard, Margaret. ed., *Letters of the American Revolution: 1774-1776*. Boston & New York: Houghton Mifflin Co., 1925.

Wright, Robert K. *The Continental Army*. Washington, D.C. Center of Military History: United States Army, 1989.

"Extract of a letter from a Rev. Divine in London dated March 3, 1766," Purdie & Dixon, *Virginia Gazette*. 23 May, 1766.

"Extract of a letter from a Gentleman in London to his friend in New York dated February 27," Purdie & Dixon, *Virginia Gazette*. 23 May, 1766.

Purdie & Dixon, *Virginia Gazette*. 20 January, 1774

Purdie & Dixon, *Virginia Gazette*. 5 May, 1774

----------- *Journals of the Continental Congress*. Library of Congress Online at www.loc.gov.

Index

About the Author

Michael Cecere Sr. is the proud father of two wonderful children, Jenny and Michael Jr., and the grateful husband of Susan Cecere. He teaches American history at Robert E. Lee High School in Fairfax County, Virginia and was named the 2006 Outstanding Teacher of the Year by the Virginia Society of the Sons of the American Revolution. Mr. Cecere also teaches American history at Northern Virginia Community College. He holds two Master of Arts Degrees from the University of Akron in both History and Political Science. An avid Revolutionary and Civil War re-enactor, he is a member of the 3rd and 7th Virginia Regiments and the Liberty Rifles, and participates in numerous living history events throughout the year. This is his fifth book. He recently published his fourth book on the role of riflemen in the American army. It is entitled: *They Are Indeed a Very Useful Corps: American Riflemen in the American Revolution.*

Other Books by Michael Cecere

They Behaved Like Soldiers: Captain John Chilton and the Third Virginia Regiment

An Officer of Very Extraordinary Merit: Charles Porterfield and the American War for Independence, 1775-1780

Captain Thomas Posey and the 7th Virginia Regiment